729

SEMINAR SPEAKING SUCCESS
Tips

David R. Portney

KALLISTI PUBLISHING
WILKES-BARRE, PA

Kallisti Publishing, Inc.
332 Center Street
Wilkes-Barre, PA 18702
Phone (877) 444-6188 • Fax (419) 781-1907
www.kallistipublishing.com

10 9 8 7 6 5 4 3 2 1

Library of Congress Control Number: 2008923340
ISBN 0-9761111-6-0
ISBN-13 978-0-9761111-6-0

DESIGNED & PRINTED IN THE UNITED STATES OF AMERICA

Dedicated to people everywhere wishing to maximize their income and success through speaking and seminars…

Table of Contents

www.AmericanSeminarAcademy.com

Why You Should Read This Book

If you're not doing seminars or some kind of public speaking, then you're just throwing away money. If you *are* doing some form of speaking, I can guarantee you're making mistakes that are costing you a lot of money and keeping you from earning what you're really worth.

Let's put it this way: **You are throwing money away because you're not doing seminar speaking right—or at all.**

Either way, you're lucky you have this book right now because these proven, real-world tips and techniques are going to save you a lot of money—and make you a lot of money.

In this book, I like to use the generic term "seminar speaking" when I talk about any kind of public speaking. I use the term "seminar speaking" to include any time you speak to a group of people. It doesn't matter whether it's an actual seminar, a workshop, or a meeting. It doesn't matter if it's a class, a boot camp, or training. It doesn't matter if it's a conference, a charity fund raising event, or a political dinner. I don't care if it's a wedding speech, a keynote speech, or a presentation to the board of directors or a group of sales prospects. If there are people there and you're speaking to them as a group, you are doing what I call *Seminar Speaking.*

If you've never done seminar speaking of any kind before, you're going to find a treasure chest full of tips, tools, and techniques here. Each tip, tool, and technique has been road-tested in the real world and proven effective—and can be put to use immediately.

If you *have* done some seminar speaking before, you're going to find some missing pieces in what you've been doing (or not doing) that will take your skill, ability, and effectiveness to a whole new level of success.

Finally, if you're a seasoned pro, you're going to be able to take these tips and put a fine shine—a high-polish—on what you're doing.

No matter what your level of experience—from rank beginner to polished professional—you're going to find in this book a practical reference guide to help you achieve smashing success with seminar speaking.

You will find inspiring tips that will motivate you to action. You will find life-saving tips that will help you conquer stage fright and overcome fear of public speaking. You will find tips that will allow you to organize your own seminars with ease. You will find tips that will allow you to prevent your seminar from becoming a chaotic disaster. You will find a number of terrific marketing tips—tips on how to get the "butts in the seats" or even get other people to do that for you. You will find tips on how to be a master of the stage and a polished and professional presenter. You will find tips on how to avoid deadly mistakes. And much more...

This book will set you on the right path. No more guesswork, no more mistakes. No more scratching your head wondering what to do. I'll separate the myths from the realities. I'll separate the lies from the truth. I'll separate the wheat from the chaff. I'll untangle fact from fiction. I'll set the record straight. In this book you get all meat—no fluff, no filler.

How To Use This Book

"Life is like a box of chocolates. You never know what you're going to get"

— Forrest Gump

This book is comprised of 129 tips. Each tip is based on my real-world experience doing literally thousands of seminars, classes, trainings, workshops, keynote speeches, presentations, and public speaking engagements for the last 26 years. These tips are not in any special order or sequence—and that's on purpose. You can open up to any page at random to find a tip you can use in the real world starting right now. The first tip listed is not first because it's meant to be read first, nor is the last tip meant to be read last.

You can treat this book like "a box of chocolates" and just open to any page and be surprised and delighted by what you find. I also think of each tip as being like a potato chip: *you can't eat just one.* Reading one tip will make you want to read another tip. The difference between this book and potato chips or chocolate is that this book is a lot less fattening. However, if you decide to use seminar speaking as a way to further your career or promote your business or sell your products and services, you will certainly make your bank account fat!

Taken altogether, the collection of tips comprises a serious body of knowledge and experience that you can put to practical use in the real world starting right away. This is not a theoretical work, nor is it a compilation of other works. You'll find that this book stands unique as compared to other works on the topic.

You'll find tips that help you to conquer stage fright. You'll find tips that help you to overcome fear of public speaking. You'll find plenty of terrific tips on how to find bookings and speaking engagements. You'll find tips on how to handle questions, tips on how to structure a flowing and flawless presentation, and tips on expert presentation skills. Taken as a whole, this book allows you to conquer stage fright, know how to organize any kind of seminar or group event, and become a master of seminar speaking.

Another way to use this book would be to pick one tip, and master that tip that day. If you choose to master one tip per day, you'll find your ability and expertise growing measurably and steadily day by day.

You may wonder why I didn't group the tips according to various themes and organize the book in a "logical" format based on different subjects such as conquering stage fright, or the logistics of doing seminars and group events, or masterful presentation skills that make you a polished pro no matter what your level of experience. While all of that is indeed in this book, I decided against grouping the tips according to subjects. This allows you as the reader to be led into the book with more of a sense of adventure. Once again, it's like a box of chocolates and you never know what you're going to get!

No matter how you read this book, I hope you'll realize that this book is not meant to be just read—*it's meant to be used*. It's meant for you to take action. If you read my book and say "What a great book!", then I will not have achieved my goal. My goal is to produce a practical book you can put to use in the real world. I hope you'll use my book this way and put it to use. Put it to the test. Make it produce real results for you that matter in your personal and professional life. Use this book to become more empowered, wealthier, and even use it to become famous, if that's what you want.

Each tip is short, to the point, concise. Don't be fooled by the brevity of each point; the brief nature of each tip is overshadowed by the power it contains. As I said, these tips come from my real-world experience of having conducted literally thousands of workshops, seminars, classes, trainings, keynote speeches, and speaking engagements of all kinds for the last 26 years. I've distilled a great deal of what I've learned through direct experience into these succinct, to-the-point nuggets of information; nuggets that are worth their weight in gold—literally!—because you can use these tips to increase your income by furthering your career, promoting your business, and selling your product or service.

In this book I use the term "seminar speaking" as a generic term for getting up in front of a group of people and talking. Seminar speaking, as I use that term in this book, includes workshops, classes, seminars, trainings, keynote speeches and speeches of any type, conferences, public speaking, boot camps, meetings, presentations—any kind of group event where you'll speak to two or more people.

The rewards of seminar speaking are virtually unlimited. You can use seminar speaking to promote your business. You can use seminar speaking to raise funds or just raise awareness. You can use seminar speaking to further political aspirations. You can use seminar speaking to sell a product or service. Seminar speaking allows you to set yourself apart from the competition and "de-commoditize" you and your business. You can use seminar speaking as a recruiting tool. You can even use seminar speaking to make yourself famous if that's what you want.

There's almost no limit to the ways you can use seminar speaking to further your personal and professional life. With seminar speaking, you can truly accelerate and explode your success!

www.AmericanSeminarAcademy.com

129 SEMINAR SPEAKING SUCCESS *Tips*

And Your Point Is...?

Before you even think about getting up in front of people and speaking or conducting a seminar, you must be 100% clear about your purpose. Are you?

Is your purpose to educate, or is your purpose to sell your product or service? Most people who want to promote their business with seminar speaking make the mistake of not being crystal clear about their purpose in advance. If your purpose is to get people to buy your product or service, design your talk to create strong desire in people to take that action.

If you want people to buy a product, use your service, or even just book an appointment with you, be 100% clear about your purpose, and know exactly what you want people to do when your talk is over. What's your purpose?

Teamwork Works!

Want a terrific way to cut your seminar costs in half?

Team up with someone that serves the same market you do, but is not a competitor. For example, if you're a real estate agent, you could team up with a loan broker or lender. Chiropractors can team up with a massage therapist. Get the idea? Just think of who serves the same market you do, and approach them to do seminars together.

That way you both split the seminar cost. If you can team up with even more people, then your costs are even less!

You Have to Aim for a Target!

Are you crystal clear about exactly who your target market is, and precisely who you want to be in front of when you do your seminar speaking?

When I ask my students "Who's your target market?", most of the time the answer is "everyone". Your target market may actually be "anyone that is breathing", but in reality, that's just too broad. You need to more tightly focus exactly who you're targeting.

Where do they live? How old are they? What's their income? Are they married or single? Do they have kids? Own their own home or rent? Do they prefer dogs or cats?

Got the idea?

You need to be so clear about exactly who your target market is that you can single them out in a crowd. When you can pick out your market just by sight, you know you've got your target right!

Your Place or Mine?

My students often ask me, "David, where's the best place to do my seminars?"

The best place to hold your seminars is the venue in which your target market will be most comfortable. Why? Because if they don't like the venue, they won't show up in the first place. To go one step further, if you're holding your seminar somewhere that your target market finds highly desirable, then you've hit the bull's-eye!

What venue will be comfortable (or even desirable) to your target market? A church? A restaurant? Country Club? Your office? Your home? Hotel banquet room?

If you're not sure, just take an informal survey and ask them!

First of All...

When you get up in front of people, what should be the very first thing that comes out of your mouth?

One school of thought is that manners never go out of style, so thank your group for being there.

Another school of thought says your opening words should be something that is so shocking that it grabs your audience by the ears and forces them to sit up & listen to you.

Why not have the best of both words? Open with a brief thank you statement and immediately follow up with your shocker/grabber question or statement.

In this case, you *can* have your cake and eat it too!

You're So Funny!

When I teach any of my workshops on Seminar Speaking Skills, inevitably someone will ask me "David, should I use humor in my seminars?"

Using humor is great because of two reasons:

1. It loosens people up, and they feel more relaxed.
2. You get a good measure of how "with you" they are.

Everyone likes to laugh (don't they?), so you create a more congenial atmosphere. Plus, you can gauge how receptive people in your audience are by noticing who's laughing.

If you are naturally funny, that's best. Never, ever try to force yourself to be funny because that will backfire on you. If you're not naturally funny, you can always work in a cartoon or funny quotation.

In the final analysis, always use your best judgment. Is humor appropriate to use with your topic and target audience?

You be the judge!

Ya Gotta Make 'Em Feel It!

Here's something that most Seminar Speakers completely miss: your seminar speaking should cause your audience to have an emotional reaction—an emotional reaction that you designed in advance.

If you want to make more money through Seminar Speaking, you *must* understand this super-important point. You're *not* trying to get your audience to have 'an understanding'.

No. Instead, you should be trying to get them to have a strong feeling, an emotional reaction. The most basic human emotions that motivate people to take action are fear (pain) and greed (pleasure).

When you touch the fear/pain and greed/pleasure of your target market audience, you're going to create a definite emotional reaction and that will motivate them to take action—the action *you* want them to take.

Step One? Check! Step Two...

Use a checklist. Use a checklist. Use a checklist.

Did I mention that you should use a checklist?

Seminars are a terrific way to promote yourself, generate more business, and make sales of your product or service.

But, seminars can also be a gigantic, painful chaotic disaster if you don't use a checklist for your seminar pre-planning, packing up, set up, and follow up.

Make one checklist for all your pre-planning, another for what you'll need to pack up and have at your seminar, one for what you want your staff to do once on-site, and one for afterwards.

That may sound like too many checklists, but believe me, after you experience what it's like to forget something major like your handouts, or to verify your booking, or some other important aspect, you'll never be without your checklist ever again!

How Did You Do?

At the end of your Seminar talk, should you pass out a feedback sheet for your audience to fill out?

The reality is, you may or may not get the truth from people. My experience is that it's hit and miss when you ask people how you can improve and similar questions.

However, a great time to use feedback sheets is when you want to capture people's contact information so you can follow up later with a special offer or sales pitch.

If you're invited to speak for a club or association, for example, you probably won't have contact info on the attendees. In that case, at the end of your talk pass out a brief, one-page "how did I do" feedback sheet with a place for them to fill out whatever contact info you'd like to collect.

Armed with their contact info, you can follow up with your free report, special offer, sales pitch, or whatever you'd like to follow up with!

Dinner Is Served?

Should you serve a meal at your seminar? Should you send out seminar invitations that offer a free breakfast, lunch, or dinner?

First, never invite the general public to a seminar where you'll serve a meal, or else you'll have a bunch of freeloaders who'll eat for free and never buy what you're selling. If your list is highly qualified (meaning you'll have a room full of good prospects in your target market), then it might make sense, but first do some math:

If it costs you $20 per head to serve a meal and you get 40 people, your meal expense alone will be $800. How much of your product or service will you need to sell just to recoup that expense? If you're in a high-commission business such as real estate, insurance, and financial planning—or if just one of your average sales will be enough to cover your meal expense—it may be worth it.

Serving a meal at a seminar can be a powerful tool for persuasion. Most people are reluctant to say "no" to your offer when they've got a mouth full of food that you've paid for.

Generally, It's Good to be Specific

Do you have "topic clarity"? What exactly is your topic? Do you know what you'll talk about when you do your Seminar Speaking?

Your first response to this question might be your general area of business, such as real estate, chiropractic, or vitamins; but that's really too general.

Ideally you should have at least *three* different topics identified. A real estate pro, for example, could have "how to save thousands of dollars on your first home purchase". (Clearly, this talk is geared to first-time home buyers and their fear of paying too much.)

As you think about *your* target market's wants and needs, what are some juicy attention-getting topics you can talk about?

Freedom of Speech?

Should you speak for free?

This question comes up in almost every workshop I teach. There are two polarized schools of thought about this.

Some say "NEVER!" while others say "speak anywhere and everywhere you can".

I've done a *lot* of both. Almost paradoxically, the more I've charged, the better behaved people have been. Free seminars may tend to attract the something-for-nothing crowd. In paid seminars, people figure "you get what you pay for".

Here's the bottom line: free seminars can be great to generate qualified prospects, but your drop-out rate will be higher and your close rate lower than with paid seminars.

In the final analysis, there's actually a time and place for both—and there's no substitute for your direct experience.

Do at least ten of each, and then measure and evaluate your results carefully. Which is producing better results for *you?*

Have a Seat...

How should you set up your seminar room and arrange seating? There are several different tried-and-true room set-ups.

Theatre style is most common, with chairs arranged in rows.

Classroom style is also common, with rows of chairs and tables.

Banquet style is often used when you're serving a meal.

Also, setting tables up in a horseshoe or "U" design is an all-purpose set up, and is great to use to give the room a full appearance when attendance is not very high.

The fastest and easiest room set up style is theatre because you can quickly add or take away chairs and rearrange rows to suit your room, your mood, and your group.

Butts in Seats

A hot topic at my workshops is marketing. Put crudely the question is "How do I get butts in seats?"

I could write an entire book on this topic. In fact, I have written a manual on Seminar Speaking Marketing. In this short space, I'll give you some valuable advice that you can start using immediately.

To start, find someone who's already doing seminars to your target market. Contact them and offer to speak at their seminar. You'll need to "sell" them on how you speaking will provide value to them.

By contacting someone who's already got the "butts in seats" and offering value to them in exchange for you speaking at their seminar, you create a true win/win situation!

Radio Station WII-FM!

Always remember this: people don't care about you.

I don't mean your family and friends don't have feelings for you. What I mean by this is that your seminar attendees for the most part don't care about your degree, your experience, your accomplishments, or how long you've been doing what you're doing. Sure, you may need to touch on that to establish your credibility, but what people *most* want to know is "What can you do for *me*!"

People only listen to one radio station: WIIFM, which stands for "What's In It For Me?". Focus your Seminar Speaking on what you can do for them, and not how wonderful you are.

Exit Stage...Fright?

Seminars are a terrific way to promote yourself, generate more business, and make sales of your product or service. So why don't more people do it?

Because of stage fright and fear of public speaking. Stage fright is the panic and fear that hits people right before they go up to speak, or when they're already speaking. Fear of public speaking is when just the thought of getting up in front of people and speaking causes them to blanch with fear.

I teach a number of highly effective, proven ways to conquer stage fright and fear of public speaking. Don't let fear stop you from reaping the huge rewards you'll get from Seminar Speaking!

Hands, Please.

When you're up in front of people doing Seminar Speaking, what should you do with your hands?

That may not sound like a big deal, but it is and here's why: Study after study has shown that non-verbal communication such as body posture and gestures has a bigger impact on your group than the actual words you say. In other words, *it's not what you say; it's how you say it!*

Avoid a lot of distracting or awkward gesturing. If you've taken my Master Seminar Speaking Training, you know there are ways to use gestures to create very specific results such as conveying trust, credibility, and expertise.

If nothing else, keep your hands at your sides, and allow yourself to make natural gestures. And yes, keep your hands out of your pockets!

Take a Hit?

Never underestimate the power of a short, introductory seminar…that *loses* money!

Too many people get stuck on "How do I make this seminar profitable?" Many times, you either can't or won't; but, a short one, two, or three hour seminar is often a great "loss leader"—which means you make money *after* the seminar.

For example, an insurance broker, real estate agent, or chiropractor may not make a single dime on the seminar, but if you take your appointment book you can schedule people for a free consultation in your office. Offer people some juicy incentive to book an appointment right then and there at your seminar.

The seminar itself becomes the first step in a two-step process of converting prospects into sales. Just one sale can often more than make up for a few "money-losing" seminars!

Show and Tell?

Should you use PowerPoint or other visual aids?

Some Seminar Speakers really overdo it; it's called "death by PowerPoint".

That said, visual aids can be a terrific help in your presentation. It's true that often "a picture is worth a thousand words." A graph or pie chart or other visual can really help you drive your point home, whether it's using a projector or just an ordinary flip chart that you draw on.

Here's my rule of thumb when it comes to visual aids: put on the screen or flip chart anything you really want them to remember.

Yes...You with Your Hand Raised...Again...

How should you handle it if you get someone in your seminar who seems to ask too many questions?

Every once in a while, you get someone in your seminar who keeps interrupting with questions. I'm making a distinction here between people asking good questions, and a disruptive person who's trying to "hijack" your seminar.

I'm generally a fan of being polite—at least to begin with. Before you resort to more "drastic measures" and have to shoot this person down, try saying "You know, you're actually out of question coupons right now. I'm sure everyone here wants to hear the rest of what I came here to speak about, so I'm going to have to answer the rest of your questions after we're done." With that said, I then go on with my presentation.

Handing a disruptive person in this manner means you stay on the good side of the group—plus, they respect you to be running the show!

Control

Ready for another strategy to handle a person that tries to "hijack" your seminar"? Stop them before they can even get started. Here's how:

Before you start into the meat of your presentation, lay down some ground rules. Make ground rule #1 something like this: "I've got a lot of great information I know you're going to be very excited to hear, so I'm going to have to ask everyone here to please hold your questions until I'm finished. I'll stay around afterwards and answer each and every question."

That way, if someone tries to hijack your seminar, you can interrupt them and say "I'm sorry, but as I mentioned before I started, you'll have to hold your questions until the end."

Some People Just Can't Take a Hint

What if you've tried the "polite methods" of handling someone who's trying to hijack your seminar, but they keep on interrupting—and just won't shut up?

Now you're going to have to resort to "more drastic measures" and shut this person down completely. But, how do you do that without turning your group against you?

Here's how: Address your group and say, "Ladies and gentlemen, I still have a wealth of information to share with you, so let's take a vote. Raise your hand if you came here to listen to him/her (no one will raise their hand) and how many came here to hear what I came here to share with you?"

The group will side with you and they'll be *very* glad you shut the disruptive person down!

Presentations on the Fly

How would you like to be able to create a dynamite presentation in no time flat, even with no time to prepare?

You have tons of great content to share with your group. But where to start? Where to finish? You're staring at a blank computer screen and don't know what to do!

Here's the answer...Put your content into this sequence: Why—What—How—What-if.

First, talk about WHY your topic is important, then cover WHAT with facts, data, and statistics, then cover HOW the group can use the information you're sharing, then cover WHAT-IF by asking your group if they have questions or by asking them questions.

By structuring the sequence of your talk in Why—What—How—What-if, you can prepare a stellar presentation quickly and easily!

It's How You Say It

Did you know that it's actually a *huge* mistake to do Seminar Speaking in your normal conversational voice?

You need to understand that people listen at three different speeds.

Fast talkers are usually fast listeners. Slow talkers are usually slow listeners. Some people listen at a more medium speed.

So, vary your speaking speed in your presentation. Speak slowly, so the slow listeners have time to digest what you're saying; speak at a more medium speed with some ups and downs in your voice; and also speak rapidly at times, so the fast listeners will be happy too. Practice varying your speaking speed in your presentation.

By speaking at three different speeds, you'll be sure to reach every listener in your group—and no one gets left behind!

Size Matters!

What's your ideal audience size? Have you given any thought to how big you want your group to be?

One thing to evaluate is your comfort level. Are you okay with speaking in front of 100 people? Or would you prefer a smaller, more "intimate" sized group?

Another aspect to evaluate is the size of your room. Also, will you need staff or other helpers if you go over a certain head-count? What about visual aids and audio needs?

The bigger your group is, the more staff, equipment, and help you're going to need. Plan accordingly!

Knowing Is Half the Battle

Do you believe that you have to know absolutely everything there is to know about your topic?

You're an expert at what you do. I know. I know…You feel you could/should know more.

First, there's always more to learn in any field. But more importantly, you don't have to know *everything* about your topic—just more than your audience does! You may not know absolutely everything there is to know about real estate or financial planning or chiropractic, but you for sure know more than your audience does! And that means you're going to have very valuable information they don't have.

Forget about the idea that you need to know everything. You only need to know more than your audience does.

Respect Mah Authoritay!

.

How do you establish your expertise and authority in the mind of your audience without appearing to be bragging?

In the workshops I teach on Successful Seminar Speaking, occasionally someone will approach me privately and ask me this question. Done properly, establishing your expertise and authority will never come across as bragging if you simply work it into your introduction. Your introduction is the place to talk about your accomplishments and abilities, your experience and your expertise.

One caveat: Be sure not to turn your entire talk into "all about you" or else it *will* be bragging!

Introducing...

What's the best way for you to be introduced? Should you do it yourself, or have someone else do it?

Personally, I've had it both ways many times, and I like both. Typically, when I'm invited to speak, someone at the event has been assigned the job of introducing me. It's a nice ego stroke hearing someone introduce me to the waiting crowd.

At many of the seminars and trainings I teach, I introduce myself—not that I can't have my staff do it, it's just my opinion that when I do it myself people see me as more accessible to them, which is something I want. I don't want them to see me as "up on a pedestal" because I want them to know they can aspire to and achieve the same level of skill I have.

Introductions really come down to a matter of personal taste. Try it both ways and see which *you* like best!

Provide a Script?

When you do Seminar Speaking, and someone is going to introduce you, should you give them a pre-written introduction?

The answer is absolutely yes!

First, you want to control what is said about you. Otherwise, who knows what they'll say! Have your introduction typed in a large, easy to read font face, double-space typed. Keep your intro to just about 1/2 of the page. (Resist the temptation to write a 5 page bio on yourself.) Keep it to the main points you want this group to know about you.

Be sure to take your introduction with you when you go. If it's not on your pre-seminar packing checklist, add it now!

Questions, Questions, Questions

Should you allow your audience to ask you questions *during* your presentation?

The answer is definitely maybe.

First you need to ask *yourself* a couple of questions. Do you have enough time to allow for questions, or should you take them after your presentation? Is your presentation designed to generate sales? If so, you need to carefully evaluate if questions could derail and ruin your flow.

In some cases, questions can contribute greatly to your presentation. In other cases, questions can completely destroy your intended result for that seminar. You'll need to be clear about the result you want to produce first, then evaluate what the impact of questions will be on that intended result.

Remember: it's *your* seminar talk, so ultimately it's up to you if you allow the audience to ask questions or not.

The Answer Is…

Strategies for handling questions:

Whenever you're asked a question by an audience member, always, always, always repeat the question. (Did I mention you should always repeat the question?) First, repeating the question aloud gives the rest of the audience a chance to hear what the question was before your start into your answer. Second, repeating the question aloud gives the person who asked the question 'validation' and they're sure that you heard the question right. Third, repeating the question gives you a slight bit of leeway time to fully consider the question and formulate an answer.

Finally, repeating questions is mandatory if you're recording your talk for future use as a promotional tool or a product!

Questions ARE the Answer

If you do allow your audience to ask questions, an excellent strategy is called "questions are the answer". If someone asks you a question, it means there's something missing from their internal representation of what you have presented. (Typically, the missing piece falls into the category of "what", "why" and most often "how" types of info.) As you repeat the question aloud, imagine that you are that person sitting in the audience who asked the question, and ask yourself what info you're missing—is it "why" info, "what" info, or "how to do it" info?

Now that you've "gotten inside the head" of that person and their question, you'll be able to provide a much better answer.

Sometimes, It's in the Cards

This just may be the absolute best way to handle questions in your seminar:

If you've decided you will take questions when you do Seminar Speaking, you still run the risk of people using the opportunity to ramble incoherently, ask questions that are completely off-topic, or even try to "hijack" or ruin your talk. Here's a terrific strategy to take questions, but completely eliminate all risk.

Take a stack of 3" x 5" blank white index cards with you. At some point, like near the beginning of your talk or before a break, tell your group that if they have any questions they'll need to write them down on the index cards you're providing. Also tell them to turn in their index cards by putting them into a box or basket you've provided, or hand them over to your assistant at the back table. You and/or your assistant can then review the questions and screen out the ones that are off-topic, nutty, or irrelevant. Then, simply pick the questions you've decided to answer and read each question aloud, then answer it.

Handling questions in this manner means that people get to ask questions, but you've removed all the risk that goes along with it!

You Gotta Stand Out!

What is your USP? Have you clearly defined your USP? Do you know what a USP is?

USP stands for **Unique Selling Proposition**. A USP is what makes you stand out from the competition. Think about it: there are a million insurance agents, financial planners, chiropractors, real estate agents...you get the idea. The trend in business is toward "commoditization". That means, in the minds of the general public, one insurance or real estate agent or chiropractor or financial planner is pretty much the same as any other. So, why should a prospect choose to do business with *you* and not someone else? If you haven't already done so, you must write down your USP right now.

Got your USP's written down? Great! Now, be sure to clearly communicate it in your Seminar Speaking!

Make 'Em an Offer They Can't Refuse

Should you make some kind of special offer when you do Seminar Speaking?

Absolutely without a doubt, YES! But what should that be?

Your special offer can take many different forms. Here are some examples to get your creative juices flowing.

If you're selling a product, you can offer it at a "this-seminar-only" discounted price. If you're promoting a service (chiropractors, real estate agents, etc.) then you can offer a free consultation in your office—but *only* if they book the appointment at your seminar. Another type of special offer is to offer them a free report on a web site you want to drive traffic to, where you sell your product(s) or service(s).

Always have some kind of "call to action" at the end of your seminar that tells them exactly what you want them to do!

Who's the Boss?

When you start your Seminar talk, it's absolutely imperative that you take control right away. Why is that so important?

If you don't take control right away, right up front, someone else probably will. I'm not talking about a desperate grab for power here, I'm talking about setting the ground rules and establishing that no one other than YOU is in charge and control.

How do you do that? I've got literally dozens of ways, but here are a few of my favorites:

1. Establish your policy on whether you will or won't be taking questions during your talk.

2. Make them do something specific, like write down their goals or introduce themselves to another person in the room.

3. Have them agree to some specific ground rule like "if you need to have a conversation with someone during my talk, please take it outside".

By setting ground rules or having them engage in specific actions you outline, you'll never run the risk of losing control of your own seminar.

Have We Got a Video?

Should you video yourself practicing a seminar talk and then watch it with an eye to how to improve?

If you open almost any "traditional" book on how to improve your speaking skills, invariably you'll hear over and over that you should video yourself and critique it with an eye to improving. But is this really, actually, in reality a good idea?

The answer is a little bit yes…and a whole lotta no.

Here's why. The little bit of yes is that you may pick out things you can and should correct, like a nervous twitch, odd postures, or distracting gestures you didn't realize you were doing. But the whole lotta no is this: if you wanted to be a karate or dance expert, and you were to video yourself, unless you were *already* an expert, your eye isn't going to be experienced, trained, and sharp enough to really know what to do to truly improve.

The only way to truly improve is under the eye of a true master of the discipline. When I conduct my Seminar Speaking Success Mastery Trainings, I personally conduct each and every minute of the training, and since I keep each training under 20 people, you get the kind of eagle-eye special attention to skyrocket your Seminar Speaking Success and skills practically overnight!

A Quick Talk Recipe

How would you like another easy formula for quickly and easily preparing your Seminar talk?

Here's a method that's tried and true. It's called "tell them, tell them, tell them". Here's how it works...

At the start of your talk, give a brief synopsis of your topic. Then, get into the "meat and potatoes" of your talk. After you've completed your talk and you've gotten to the end of your subject matter, then give a bullet-point summary of the main points of your talk. Because people's minds tend to wander at various points of your talk, this strategy makes sure that everyone is totally clear on the important points you most want to get across.

Remember, when you want to make sure your group gets the most important points of your talk, just tell 'em, tell 'em, tell 'em!

I Once Caught a Fish THIS BIG!

Should you make outrageous claims in your seminars?

Making outrageous claims will definitely get people's attention. I don't know about you, but I've heard a lot of boastful claims at seminars. For example, I've heard a lot of wild claims of huge income or sales. Funny, though, they never seem to be able to back up those claims with any tangible proof!

If you're going to make claims in your Seminar Speaking—even if they're not outrageous claims—you should be able to provide tangible proof. If you don't provide solid proof for your claims, doubts will linger in the back of people's minds, and your credibility will suffer—and so will your sales.

Don't make any claims you can't back up with solid, irrefutable evidence. Better yet, provide a mountain of proof!

39

Track Your Results

If you can't measure your results, you have no real results.

Over the years, I've literally conducted many thousands of workshops, seminars, talks, presentations, and trainings. I've done them in-town, out-of-town, and all over the country. I've had audiences of only three people and I've had rooms with many hundreds of people. I've done seminars at night, in the morning, on weekdays, and on weekends. I've done seminars in each and every month of the year, year-in, year-out. Along the way, I've kept data and statistics on many details.

You know what always gives me a good laugh? It's when I've heard self-proclaimed seminar experts spouting-off about the best and worst days/weeks/months to do seminars, but they have very little, or even nothing, tracked and written down. I once heard someone say "measurement eliminates argument" and I agree. The best data is that which is tracked in writing, not from memory. If you track the vital statistics about your seminar, you accumulate vital data you can review later for trends. That way you can do more of what's working, and less of what's not working!

The moral of the story is *always track your results*. Later, you'll be glad you did.

Every Day Is a Good Day

What are the best days of the week to do seminars?

The shortest possible answer—and the most correct answer—is *every day of the week*.

How is that possible? Because every day of the week is perfect depending on your target market. Suppose your target market is working class people who work 9-5, Monday to Friday. If you offer them a seminar on a weekday in the middle of the work week, you'll probably get some people who'll show up, but don't you think your attendance is likely to be better on the weekend? What if your target market is hard-core football fans, do you think a Sunday during football season will pull very many people who want to hear you talk?

When you want to schedule a seminar, carefully consider your target market's schedule and routines. Schedule your seminars on days that are most likely to be good for them, not necessarily the days that are good for you. That way you stand the chance to get the best turnout, and get better exposure and sales.

When it comes to Seminar Speaking, it's been my direct experience that every day is a good day for a seminar.

Your Elevator Pitch

What is your elevator speech and your elevator pitch?

Most likely, you've heard of an elevator speech, right? The elevator speech is simply this, suppose you're in an elevator, and someone asks you what your business is, in 10-20 seconds what would you say to best sum up and encapsulate what you do in an enticing, interest-generating way? Of course, you should develop and polish your elevator speech. Maybe you already have. But have you also developed and polished your elevator pitch?

If you only had 10, 20, or maybe 30 seconds at the most, how could you not only give an enticing explanation of what you do, but also "pitch" them on you giving a talk on your topic? The key to a great elevator pitch is to tie what you do into the needs and/or wants of the person and/or their business. For example, can you help them to improve employee productivity? Cut expenses? Boost sales and revenues? Improve profitability?

A polished elevator pitch should not only encapsulate what you do, but also explain how you can benefit them and/or their business directly.

If...Then

Are you consistently using a "conditional close"?

More and more, we're inundated with sales pitches. It's starting to seem like we're bombarded with sales messages from the moment we wake up until the moment we go to sleep. Hopefully, advertisers won't figure out how to advertise in our dreams. Many of us have become jaded if not immune to "sales techniques", especially some of the more well-known and over-used techniques such as the "forced choice close"—"Would you like it in blue or red?" or "Would you like to meet on Tuesday morning or Thursday afternoon?"

When it comes to sales techniques, an oldie but goodie that you should be using consistently is the "conditional close". It goes like this: "If I can X, will you Y?" That's the basic structure. You always want to tie your conditional close into a specific want or need on the part of your prospect. For example, "If my seminar can measurably boost employee morale and productivity, would you book me right away?" Now, that's just one small example, but you get the idea, right?

I suggest you practice using the conditional close until it becomes second nature.

The Lazy Man's Way to Get Butts in Seats

Want a quick and easy way to get "butts in seats" for your seminar?

Let someone else do it. More specifically, approach someone who already does it. Even more specifically, approach the clubs in your area that hold regular meetings and offer to speak to their members at their next meeting. For free.

With very little effort on your part, you can turn up at least half a dozen clubs right in your back yard: Kiwani's, Rotary, Lion's, American Legion, Veteran's, and singles clubs are just a few that you'll find in your area. Then there's all the special interest clubs such as diving, sailing, rock climbing, art appreciation, quilting, real estate investing...Got the idea? These clubs are always on the lookout to provide value to their members.

Don't worry if you can't speak on rock climbing or quilting! In fact, often they're more interested in hearing a speaker talk about a different topic, especially if you can tie what you do into their club member's interest in a clever or unique way.

When it comes to getting butts in seats, this is the "lazy man's way". Let someone else do it!

Go For the Body, Rocky!

Did you know that every time you do a talk, you should hit people in the gut? Don't worry. I'm not saying you should punch people in the stomach. In fact, don't do that!

What I am saying, is that there are three main ways to affect and influence people: their head, heart, and gut. I'm suggesting that if you want to influence people in a profound way, you need to get them to have a gut-level reaction. How? By making sure that in your talk you appeal to their emotions.

Appealing to logic and reason won't accomplish that goal. Only emotions will create a gut-level reaction in your audience. You can determine for yourself what kind of emotions you'd like to stir in your group, but I'm going to suggest that by far the number one emotion that will cause your group to have a strong emotional reaction (and act on it) is fear. Some say people are moved more by pain than pleasure, but pain is a direct feeling in your body. Pain is not an actual emotion. However, fear of future pain *is* an emotion—a very strong emotion.

Hit people in the gut with fear of future pain, and how you can save them from that pain; but please, be able to really help them.

Meet, Greet, and Be Happy!

Want yet another good strategy to mitigate any pre-talk jitters?

If you've taken any of my workshops and trainings, you know that I help people to conquer stage fright and eliminate fear of public speaking. People manage to "create" stage fright in a number of ways, but a very common way is to look out over an audience, and feel the eyes of a bunch of staring strangers burning a hole in them. Yikes! Who wouldn't feel uncomfortable with all those eyes burning holes in them?! Here's how to prevent that from ever happening to you.

Arrive early before your talk and make time to walk around and meet some of the audience members. Introduce yourself as the speaker, thank them for coming, ask them some targeted questions about what they're hoping to hear about. Be genuinely friendly and curious. It will feel good to talk to these people. Then, when you're "on stage", be sure to make eye contact with your new "friends" consistently. Heck, if it's a small group, you may even be able to meet everyone before you start your talk.

Meeting people and being friendly before you start your talk means these people are not strangers boring holes in you. They're your new friends.

Bad Days

"Successful Seminar Speakers don't have bad days"
— David Portney

The above quote is to illustrate one simple point: *When you're a Seminar Speaker, you have to deliver.*

Now, you may have just gotten the worst haircut of your life, just received a parking ticket, just spilled coffee on your shirt, just found out that your dog ate your sofa and your cat has ripped up the drapes and your bird flew away…but you have to deliver to your audience! You can't get up in front of people and start moaning and complaining to them. Don't you think they have enough problems of their own? Why should they want to hear yours?

Now, if you're funny about the coffee stain on your shirt, then you and everyone else has a good laugh, and you move on. But if you come across as grouchy and complainy, you're not going to fare very well with people.

Remember, when you're a Seminar Speaker, you don't have bad days.

Let Other People Sell You!

How can you convince people that they should buy your product, use your service, and do business with you?

People are becoming more and more resistant to sales pitches. But, at some point, you have to ask people for the sale, right? At some point, you have to try to "close" them, don't you? What if you could get other people to do the closing for you? Would that make your job easier?

Here's how: **client testimonials.**

Let's say you're near the end of your talk, and you want to "close them" on the idea of doing business with you. You reach to the side table and pull out a thick stack of paper. "Let me share just a few of the comments I've gotten from my clients over the years…" You then read three or four earth-shaking, heartfelt, rock-their-world testimonials from your satisfied clients (of course, get their permission ahead of time). The audience starts to wonder if you're going to read the whole huge stack of testimonials, so you toss the stack aside and say, "I just don't have enough time to read all these to you" and you proceed to make your special offer.

When it comes to "closing" people on doing business with you, why not let other people do it for you?

Create a Human Connection

What is your TPS? Do you know what a TPS is?

TPS stands for Tell (a) Passionate Story. Here's why you need at least one good TPS.

When you get in front of people and speak, you need to create a bond of rapport and affinity with them. If they've never met you before, then you're a stranger to them. Why should they care about you? Why should they believe you? Why should they trust you?

When you tell a true, passionate, real-life story from your past, it hooks people in. They put themselves in your place as you relate the details of your story. It creates a human connection between you and your audience. They relate to you. That connection you create means that people see you as being more like them, and not just "some person up there speaking". In fact, afterwards, some people will probably tell you how moved they were by your story, and how much they related to it.

TPS means people see you as more real, they feel a human connection with you, and they're more likely to believe you—and therefore do business with you.

Junk...Errr...Direct Mail

Should you use direct mail to promote a seminar?

Direct mail, of course, is mailing out seminar invitations to your target market. Is this a good idea?

Direct mail is a tricky affair. You can easily spend thousands of dollars on printing and postage, with absolutely zero guarantee you'll get even one response. Many people have successfully used direct mail to fill their seminars. It's a tried and true method, but it can get very expensive, very quickly. Some extremely important factors to consider are, the quality of the mailing list you use, the specific mailing piece form (postcard, letter, etc.), how compelling the sales copy is, and what your budget is. Another super important factor is the total dollar amount of your average sale and how many projected sales you can reasonably make at your seminar.

Direct mail campaigns can work well if you have a great list, great mailing piece and copy, and will earn large dollar amounts on even one sale. If you're selling a $19.95 book, does it make sense to spend $5,000 or more in direct mail? However, high commission industries such as insurance, real estate, and financial planning can do very well because even one sale can result in many thousands of dollars earned.

A Room Full of Eager People

Are you ready for another great way to have a room full of people eager to hear your talk and receive your message?

One simple word: **associations**.

Associations are organizations with a membership comprised of one specific interest or industry. There are associations for every interest and industry you can think of—and a whole lot you can't. There are associations for real estate agents, insurance brokers, chiropractors, jugglers, auto enthusiasts, financial advisors, dog lovers…you name it.

Contact associations that serve your niche market and offer to speak to their members at an upcoming meeting. They'll be thrilled to hear from you because they have to constantly justify the fees they charge their members and provide value to those members. You are providing them with a quick and easy (and perhaps even free) way for them to provide yet more value to their membership list.

But, how do you find these associations, you ask? Easy! Just go to your local public library and ask the librarian for the *Gale Encyclopedia of Associations*.

Just like clubs, associations are a terrific way to speak to groups in your target market. Start making contact today!

Good Month/Bad Month

Here's another common question I get at the seminars and workshops I teach on Successful Seminar Speaking: "David, are there good and bad months during the year to do seminars?"

This is a hotly contested issue among the experts. Some say that attendance at seminars is down during summer vacation months and the November-December holiday season. So they call those bad months. Others say those months are the perfect months to do seminars because everyone else won't be doing seminars, so you'll have no competition.

As you already know, I'm a big fan of tracking my results, so I have more than an opinion about it. I have actual facts to back up what I say. As I look at my data from years of conducting various kinds of seminars, I've seen attendance take a dip during summer and holiday months, and take an upswing in the beginning of the year, Spring, and again in September. But that's speaking *generally* because I've had classes two weeks before Christmas that were standing room only when I expected little or no turnout!

My bottom line is this: don't avoid doing seminars during so-called "bad months" just because someone else said so. There's no substitute for testing and your direct experience over time. *Your* seminar may pull huge crowds during the so-called bad months. Test and find out!

Tapping into Your Passion?

Passion captivates people. When others see someone feeling intensely about something, that gets noticed—in a big way. Even if they don't agree, they still notice and remember the intensity of passion expressed. Are you expressing passion in your seminar talk?

The power of passion is something you should definitely use to your advantage. Why do you do what you do? What's your purpose, your mission? What drives you? Share that with your group. It doesn't matter whether you're a real estate broker, insurance agent, chiropractor, plumber, or financial advisor; key into your purpose, your mission, your drive and share that with others. Tell your group about it.

People respond to those who are passionate. People are moved my passion. People are influenced by passion. Passion is contagious.

Tap into your passion by tapping into your sense of purpose and mission, then share your passion. Let your light shine bright!

Any Time Except Late for Dinner

If you're going to schedule a short introductory or free seminar, what's the best time of day to do it?

If you answered, "The time of day that works best for my target market," then I'm going to give you a nice pat on the back.

What time of day do you suppose is going to be best for retired senior citizens? Do you think an evening or morning seminar will pull better? How about working parents? Do you think a Saturday or Sunday morning seminar will get you very many real estate agents? How about chiropractors?

Always think from the point of view of your target market, and if you're not sure, just ask them!

Generally, It Pays to be Specific

In your seminar talk, how specific can you be?

During the "what" portion of your seminar, you're going to share facts, data, and statistics. Those facts and data are going to outline the problem you solve and/or the solution itself. In this case, being specific is much more powerful than being general. For example, let's say in your talk about smart college funding, you talk about how much money you can save parents. Instead of saying "You'll save about $5,000," notice how much more believable it sounds if you say "The average savings you'll enjoy will be $5,327.48." Of course, I'm not suggesting you make up fake numbers to support your talk; you should always give out real facts. But most speakers tend to round off those real numbers, when it's actually much better to quote the specific amount down to the penny.

Being specific is much more powerful than being general. How specific can you be?

Keep It Simple...
(You Know the Rest)

A confused person will always say "No!"

After all the work, time, and effort you put into designing your seminar talk, setting up the seminar, and handling the many details to get in front of a group of people and promote your business, don't ruin all that by confusing people. In a case like this where you're communicating to a group of people, *clarity is key.* The purpose of your seminar is (or at least should be!) to get those people to take some specific action. Does your talk clearly communicate exactly what action you want people to take? Do you want them to be convinced about something? Do you want them to buy something? Do you want them to make an appointment with you? What exactly do you want them to do?

Here's the test of whether you're being clear or confusing. Give a shortened version of your talk to a twelve year old child. Do they clearly understand what your talk is about and what action you're suggesting they take? If not, rework it until it's 100% clear.

When people are confused, they pull back and they don't take action. Don't ruin all the time and effort you put into your seminar talk by confusing people. Make sure even a twelve year old child can understand!

Even Dr. Frankenstein Had Igor!

Do you have someone that can help you with the details of your seminar?

I've done so many seminars over the years, I can handle the myriad details almost in my sleep. But if you're relatively new to setting up and delivering seminars, you'll quickly find that there seems to be a million details that have to be handled. Plus, the timing of all those details must be carefully coordinated. There are details before your seminar—getting invitations out, handling phone registrations, preparing the handouts, *etc.* Then there are all the details at the seminar location—equipment set up and testing, handling incoming attendees and so on. Even after the event, there is equipment breakdown and packing, following up with attendees, counting up the sales (hopefully!) and so forth.

Are you prepared to handle all that by yourself? Especially in the beginning when you want to concentrate most of your time and energy on your presentation, you would do well to find people to help you with details.

OPD (Other People's Databases)

Conducting seminars is not rocket science, but there are many, many details to attend to. A critical piece is how exactly are you going to promote your seminar, thereby getting a group of people to make your presentation to?

If you're promoting a seminar date you have set up, it comes down to a numbers game: the more people you invite, the more attendees you potentially will have. Again, not rocket science. But—and this is a big *but*—what if you don't have a large list of people whom you can contact to promote your seminar?

Here are three important words: **Other People's Databases**.

Who do you know that already has a large list you can potentially contact with your seminar invitation? Start with people you know who naturally have large lists of clients, such as your CPA, lawyer, chiropractor, real estate agent, insurance agent and so forth. They'll likely have large lists you can reach out to. Where appropriate (and legal!) offer them part of the registration fee for each attendee you get as a result of tapping into their database. 50% of each registration dollar is not too much to pay.

Utilizing other people's databases is very cost effective for you because you only pay out for people that actually have paid to attend!

The Most Important Question

Do you know what question may just be the world's most powerful question? Probably the world's most powerful question, is this:

"What's important to you about _____?"

By now, you should have already clearly defined your target market, but do you *really* know what's important to them? Many seminar speakers (and business owners) presume and assume they already know, but when was the last time you actually asked them? Asking this question can give you information you would never have known otherwise. When you ask your target market this question, listen very closely to the answer. You may be surprised by what you find out! You may discover new information or you may find out you're already right on track. Never assume you already know what they want.

Ask your target market what's important to them, then make sure to weave that into your seminar talk, and you'll be sure to be hitting their "hot buttons".

"I Love Technology... When It Works!"

I do love technology. I hate when it doesn't work, though. But, that's the nature of things. Sometimes they stop working —and sometimes for no reason. Unfortunately, sometimes technology stops working at exactly the wrong time. So of course, it will happen to you too.

What will happen? You'll have a terrific PowerPoint presentation up on the screen...and the projector or laptop will fail. Or maybe you're using even more modern equipment...and it fails. I've seen many a seminar speaker completely fall apart when this happens.

But, I always have a printed outline of my talk whenever I do a seminar. That way, even if the power fails, I can still deliver my presentation. You need to do the same thing: *always have a back-up plan.* You should be able to deliver a stellar presentation, even if technology decides to stop working.

You should never fall apart if technology fails. Just reach over to your handy outline and seamlessly keep going with your seminar talk!

You Must Have BOR!

Do you have BOR?

BOR stands for **Back Of** (the) **Room**, and refers to products being sold at the back table of your seminar. Sometimes referred to as "back-end products" or just "back-end", the products you sell at your seminar can represent a sizable amount of revenue. You should not ignore BOR, even if you don't have a "product-based" business.

Any business—including strictly service-based businesses like chiropractors, real estate agents, and financial advisors—can and should have BOR. You should be selling your book, audio program, or DVD. If you don't have any products yet, you can always find products that fit your business and purchase a license to sell those products. (If you do that, be sure that the product does not compete for the business you're trying to generate at your seminar!)

Many Seminar Speakers make little or no money on the actual seminar itself, but rake in huge profits from BOR. No matter what business or industry you're in you can, you should, and you *must* have BOR.

BOR Products the Easy Way

Want an easy way to create BOR (Back Of the Room) products you can sell at your seminar?

If you get a license to sell someone else's products, that's fine, but it's better if you have *your own products* to sell. First, you get to keep all the profits for yourself. Just as important, your products only promote you, your business, your brand, your message. Your products are unique to *you.*

But how do you create products quickly, easily, and without a lot of costs and expenses? Books are great, but can take time to produce. DVD's can be expensive to produce unless you're already good at video production and editing.

However, recording audio is easy, inexpensive, and fast. You can easily buy an affordable and good microphone that plugs right into your computer. Standard software will allow you to edit and burn your very own audio CD's. For a couple of hundred dollars, packaging companies will duplicate, package, and shrink-wrap your product. If you're selling BOR at your seminar, you don't need to worry about getting a bar code, just affix a price tag of $19.95, or whatever your price is.

Recording audio products is the least expensive way to produce quality BOR quickly and easily.

Practice, Man, Practice

Should you rehearse your seminar talk before you deliver your presentation to a "live" group?

Traditional, conventional wisdom you can find in any library book on public speaking will typically say yes. However, if you are going to rehearse, let me give you some important pointers.

First, rehearsal can help you to feel more prepared when you give your actual talk. Conventional wisdom says that rehearsal and preparation will help ease any nervousness you may feel. That's good. One thing you don't want to do, however, is rehearse in order to memorize your talk, because you'll probably come across as "stiff" and "scripted".

I'd like to suggest that if you're going to rehearse your talk, here's a twist that will really ease any jitters and nervousness: when you rehearse, practice delivering your presentation with as much confidence as you can possibly muster. Recalling times in your past when you felt supremely confident can help bring up loads of confidence. Practice your talk feeling strong levels of confidence. That way you create a link between giving your talk and strong feelings of confidence. Then, by creating that link between giving your talk and strong feelings of confidence, you'll feel that strong confidence when you do your actual Seminar Speaking!

You Are What You...Emulate

How would you like to become a more powerful, more dynamic, more effective Seminar Speaker almost instantly?

Here's how...First, think of a speaker who has the kind of qualities you wish you had. This person could be someone you've seen on TV, or in church, or in a seminar you once attended. If you want, you can even go to the library and get videos of various public figures such as past presidents giving powerful presentations.

Once you've decided on someone, observe them closely. How do they use their voice? How do they gesture? How do they stand? How do they move? What is their posture like? Observe closely what they do with their face, voice, gestures, and body posture. You can even write down some notes about what you discover and observe.

Next, play a game of trying to be just like them. Practice small parts of your presentation while trying to be just like them. For fun, have a friend or relative observe and help "mold you" into being just like the person you're emulating. They can even offer feedback on what's powerful and effective.

When you emulate powerful, dynamic, effective speakers you'll begin to take on some of those qualities. Try it right now!

It's in the Way That You Use It

How many different ways can you use seminars? How many ways do you want to use seminars?

It's pretty common for people to get locked into a single mindset when it comes to ways of doing seminars. What does that mean? It means that often people think of seminars as something they can use for one purpose and one purpose only.

As an example, take someone who does a sales seminar. They pretty much limit themselves to that kind of seminar, and only that kind of seminar. But in reality, there are so many uses for seminars I could fill up an entire book with just that.

Here's some examples to get your creative juices flowing: Client appreciation seminars, client education seminars, introductory seminars, charity fund raising seminars, award banquet seminars, seminars to raise people's awareness about a certain cause or issue, seminars to recruit employees, seminars to further a political candidate, seminars to make yourself well-known or even famous, and of course, seminars to promote your product, your service, and your business.

How many different ways can *you* think of to use seminars?

A Little Oil for the Gears

Here's a little tip to help make your seminars go just a little bit more smoothly.

I don't know where you plan to hold your seminars. But if you're doing your own seminars, as opposed to speaking at someone else's events, you're going to have to deal with every aspect—planning, set up, delivery, breakdown, follow-up...everything. You may be doing your seminar at a church, restaurant, hotel room, or other venue.

Wherever you do hold your seminar, plan on having a minimum of three tables available to you and your staff. Have one table at the front of the room for you and your needs (your outline, your laser pointer, testimonial letters, *etc.*). Have a second table just inside or just outside the entry way to your seminar room to be used as a registration table. Have a third table set up at the back of the room to hold products for sale, brochures, name tags, and things like that.

If you need more tables for various other needs, be sure to arrange for them as well, but you should plan ahead on having at least three tables available to you.

Be sure to communicate to your venue ahead of time of your need for tables. Also, let your staff know what they are for.

Needs Vs. Wants

Have you fully considered what your target market needs versus what your target market wants?

Everyone has needs and wants. Some basic human needs are food, water, shelter and sleep. Some basic human wants are belonging, meaning, and purpose. We could argue about what humans really need or want, but the question here is, are you clear about what your target market needs and wants, and which motivates them more strongly?

If you're a chiropractor, you may know that your patients need regular adjustments, but your patients are more likely interested in wanting to be pain-free. If you're a financial planner, you may know that people need to invest for retirement, but people may want to not be penniless in their golden years.

There is a definite difference between needs and wants, and you need (and should want) to find out your target market's needs and wants—and figure out which motivates them more strongly.

Armed with the facts about your target market's needs and wants be sure to integrate that into your seminar talk.

The Inevitable Conclusion

Are you afraid to ask for the sale? It's been my experience that business people are good at talking about the features and benefits of what they have to offer, but when it comes to asking for the sale, people start to get shy.

Why is that? You believe in your product or service, don't you? I've noticed over the years that people start to get shy when it comes to asking for payment—money. Could it be that the reason some get shy about asking for the sale is because it's the same as asking for money?

Now, in a seminar, you can ask for the sale directly. I know someone who does this by asking "So, do you want it or what?" Pretty direct.

But, one of the beautiful things about doing seminar speaking is that you don't have to ask for the sale directly. Instead, you can make your seminar talk lead your group to the **inevitable conclusion** that they need your product or service. That means that your audience hears what you have to say and make the conclusion in their mind that they simply must have your product or service.

Afraid to directly ask for the sale? Then just lead your group to the inevitable conclusion that they have to have what you're selling.

After the Show...

Are you making yourself accessible after your seminar talk? What do you do after your seminar talk?

If you're like most seminar speakers, you hang around to answer questions and chat with your seminar attendees. Most seminar speakers hang around the front of the room to do that. I think that's a bad idea.

It's a good idea to be accessible after your talk, but not at the front of the room. It's likely that at your seminar you'll have a table at the back of the room with products for sale or, at a minimum, brochures and information you want your attendees to leave with. I suggest that somewhere near or at the very end of your talk, you announce that you'll be at the back of the room to answer questions. Then, when you're done, head straight for the back of the room without delay. Someone will try to stop you and ask you a question, but don't stop and answer their question there because soon you'll have a crowd of people around you wanting to ask their question, and you'll be stuck. When someone tries to stop you, just remind them you'll be taking questions at the back of the room and keep moving. Then, stand either directly behind your back-end table, or certainly right next to it, so that your natural draw pulls people there.

Murphy Was an Optimist

Would you like a simple yet effective way to be ready in case you lose your seminar outline and technology fails?

Imagine that despite your best preparations, somehow you are in a bad situation. You're about to give your seminar talk, but you can't make your prepared presentation because of technology problems. On top of that, you can't find the backup outline of your seminar talk! Yikes! You're going to have to wing it and improvise!

Well, don't panic, because I've got a simple yet very effective solution for you. Just get up and speak about the problems your product or service solves. Think of your "emergency talk" as having two distinct parts:

Part one is defining and outlining the problem and part two is about how you can solve those problems. No matter what your product or service—no matter what line of business you're in—you're really in the problem-solving business. When you think about it, no matter what you do, you're solving a problem people have. Stop and think about what problems you solve.

If you wind up with no way to deliver the presentation you prepared, at least you'll have an emergency back up plan that can't fail.

Your Worst Nightmare

What's the absolute worst thing you can imagine happening during your seminar talk? You might not want to think about it. You might prefer to try to bury that thought of that one thing that's so horrible that if it happened during your seminar talk, you'd completely fall apart. No, I'm not a sadist. So why am I rubbing your nose in your greatest fear?

It's because very often that thing we fear needs to have the "sting" taken out of it just in case. In reality, that thing you fear so much either will never happen or is just something you've built up in your mind and blown it out of proportion. Often, we can defuse that worst case scenario by exposing it to the light of day, finding something funny about it, or even making fun of it.

What do you imagine as being the absolute worst thing you can imagine happening during your seminar? Go ahead, expose it. Now, what's actually funny about it? Think up three ways you could turn that into a joke if it were to actually happen. Give yourself permission to completely alleviate and relieve yourself of that fear. Unburden yourself today!

You're in the Director's Chair!

As the leader of your seminar, you are like a Hollywood director. When you do your own seminars, you're the star of the show, but you're also the director.

Seminars require careful coordination of many details. I suggest that you sit down and decide ahead of time exactly what roles your assistants or staff will perform.

Clearly outline what duties need to be performed and exactly who will handle each of those duties. Who will be responsible for registering participants on a sign-in sheet as they arrive? Who exactly will be responsible for introducing you? Who will handle taking payments for sales you make at your seminar? Who will set up the room, the projector, arrange the chairs and tables? Who will be responsible for packing up all your gear afterwards? Who will be accountable for making appointments for people to see you in your office next week? Who will be responsible for communicating and coordinating with the venue and their staff?

Remember, you're the director. It's up to you to figure out how to handle it when it comes to "lights, camera, action!"

It Slices! It Dices!

Have you considered if you'll give some kind of demonstration as part of your seminar talk?

Demonstrations can have a huge impact on a crowd. For example, during my *Seminar Speaking Success Mastery* trainings, I'll bring at least one person up front and lead them through what I call "The Hero Process"—a sure-fire method of instantly improving your seminar speaking skill. You should see the looks on people's faces when they see someone go from mouse to lion in a few seconds flat! Or go from "passable" to powerful.

You get the idea. By doing a demonstration, people have what's called an "a-ha!" moment. They have a transformative moment where they realize that they can benefit the exact same way as the person they just watched at the front of the room. And, it creates desire. Of course, I always risk that my demo won't work, but you can take a suggestion from me and always keep going until your demo does work.

Can you do some kind of demonstration in your seminar to create a transformative moment in your audience?

Whose Want Are You Offering?

Are you offering people what they want *or* are you offering people what you want them to want?

Coca Cola markets carbonated sugar water; do people really need that? No, but they have learned to want it. Now, you may not think drinking carbonated sugar water is a good idea, but what if your target market wants it? It's common for someone to write a book or start a business without checking to see if anyone wants what they're offering.

Recently, a local company started offering small propane tank delivery for barbecues, outdoor lighting and such. But no one around here really wanted propane tanks delivered, so they went out of business. I'm sure that the guys who started the company thought it was a good idea or else they wouldn't have launched the business. And, I'm positive they wanted people to want what they were offering. But people didn't want that.

How does this apply to your seminar speaking? In your talk, are you offering what people want or what you want them to want?

Hotel, Motel, Holiday Inn

Hotel meeting and banquet rooms are always a good choice for a seminar venue. Sure, you're going to spend some money, but often it's going to be worth it. Hotels are a neutral, "safe" environment for people. Most hotels have meeting rooms and all the items and equipment you could want. It's cheaper to own your own projector and other basic seminar equipment, but if you don't have it, they probably will.

Talk to the staff in the banqueting and catering department to see if you can get the room for free if you serve an inexpensive buffet. If you don't want to serve a meal, you can still get a very good room without having to take out a mortgage on your house. Remember that you should choose a hotel that is appropriate to both your target market as well as your industry. Typically, the more expensive your product or service, the nicer the hotel has to be.

Check on rates and availability well in advance of your seminar date. Once they quote you a price for a room, then ask, "I see, but what are your corporate rates?"

Also, check around for your local "business" hotels. You can often get a much lower price on your seminar room there.

Your Rock of Gibraltar

Your mental state is tremendously important when it comes to your Seminar Speaking Success every time you get up in front of people and speak. Why? Because people are going to pick up on your mental state. It's not magic, and it's not telepathy. It's just simply the fact that your mental state is going to be reflected in your facial expressions, your body posture, and your voice tone. You can try and hide or cover up a bad mental state, but in most cases, it won't work. So what's the answer? If you're in a bad state and you're about to get up and speak, what should you do?

I suggest you have a certain something you can draw on in a time of need. That certain something is some kind of strength you can draw on. Perhaps you have a strong religious faith. Or perhaps you can draw on a past experience when you were able to overcome seemingly insurmountable obstacles. Or maybe you have particularly strong family ties.

Virtually everyone has some rock-solid foundation they can call on when they need strength and resolve. What's your "Rock of Gibraltar"?

Repetition...Repetition...

Repetition is the key to success. Repetition is the key to success. Repetition is the key to success.

Have I ever mentioned the fact that repetition is the key to success?

Two critical points here: one is the fact that you can't become a violin virtuoso or a black belt in Judo by taking one or two lessons. Repetition is the key to success. It's the same with seminar speaking success—if you only do it once or twice then give up, you're probably not going to see the kind of results and success you want.

The second critical point is this: in your seminar talk, always be sure to repeat the key points you most want people to remember. Repeat the key points.

Repeating the key points means people will remember them. Get the idea? I think you do!

Have I ever mentioned to you that repetition is the key to success?

So, You're New...

"I've never done this before..."
"This is my first time doing this..."
"Normally, I don't do this kind of thing..."

I realize that you think you're getting sympathy from people because you're nervous and jittery about your first few seminar talks. So you confess you're a complete newbie. But your confession won't ease your stage fright. It just won't.

Furthermore, you may get one or two people who sympathize with you, but you do more damage than good. The most common response in people's minds is "Then why are you up there speaking?" as they roll their eyes. If you had a plumber show up at your house to fix your toilet, how would you feel if he said "This is my first time doing this"? You'd wish you'd called another plumber, someone experienced who knows what they're doing, right?

Your audience is there on a "need-to-know-basis" and they don't need to know if you're a rookie seminar speaker.

Promising the World

Can you make some huge, hard-to-believe promise, and then deliver on it?

If you can make a huge promise people find difficult to believe is true, but can back it up, you're going to really grab people's attention. For example, I can take someone who rates their stage fright at 10 out of 10, and reduce it to a level 5 or below in five minutes or less. That's a pretty big promise, but I can back it up.

What kind of huge promise can YOU make that you can back up? Can you show people how to be pain free in less than ten minutes? Can you show people how they can go from deep in debt to debt-free in 90 days?

I don't know what business you're in, but you do, so think about what kind of huge promise you can make that you can deliver on and convert the skeptics in the crowd.

You can make a quite an impact on your group with a huge, hard-to-believe promise. Imagine their reaction when you back it up!

Make a Storyboard

Do you have a lot of material you plan to deliver in your seminar talk, but you're wondering how you're going to organize it all?

Here's a time-tested technique that works like a charm. Get a nice big stack of index cards. One at a time, write down a major point on your index cards. Then, just lay them all out on the floor and begin to arrange them in the order and sequence that makes the most sense. If you need to change the sequence, just change the cards around. Move the index cards around until you arrive at a sequence that you like most. If you want, you can do the same thing with those yellow sticky notes that you can buy at any office supply store, and arrange them on a large table or even a wall.

This technique is actually called "storyboarding" and is used in the movie making process to line up the various scenes and takes in a movie.

When you're not sure how to sequence a large amount of seminar material, just take a clue from Hollywood and use storyboarding.

Punctuality

Should you start and end your seminar punctually and exactly on time, every time?

Conventional wisdom says yes, but I've broken that rule many, many times. I admit it. Why? Well, occasionally I've gotten a little carried away and forgotten to pay attention to time and run overtime. People nicely let me know by rustling papers and squirming in their seats.

I've also started late, but the only reason I've ever done that is because of waiting for some people to show up that were just minutes away, or pulling into the parking lot.

Having said that, I'm more than willing to agree with conventional wisdom and say yes, it's a good idea to start and end on time. If you're going to break the rule like me and start a little late, ask the group (if it's a small group) if they think you should wait a few minutes for the rest of the group.

Ultimately, you're the boss of your seminar and you can do whatever you want, but at the risk of seeming hypocritical, I'll side with conventional wisdom on this one.

Wake 'Em & Shake 'Em!

How do you "wake up" your group and get them to pay attention when you want to get an important point across?

No matter how great a speaker you are—no matter how captivating and powerful you may be—it's inevitable that people's minds are going to start to wander. So, when you want everyone's attention—*your entire audience*—to be completely riveted on an important point you're making, how do you shake them out of their daze?

Here's what you should do. Simply raise the volume of your voice and point with your index finger. You can point at the ground, or for a really dramatic effect, point directly at the audience. Pointing at the ground is less dramatic, but still works very well. Feel free to use a "stabbing motion" with your pointing finger to mark out the specific words or phrase you want them most to absorb at that moment. In the extreme you can even be yelling at that point, but that's not usually necessary.

So, when you need to "wake 'em up and shake 'em up" to get your point across, just raise your voice and point! You can see me demonstrate this on video at *www.SeminarAcademy.com.*

And Suddenly It Strikes...

What if you're up in front of people speaking, and you have a sudden, unexpected attack of stage fright?

That's a question I've been asked countless times in my seminars and workshops. If you have a sudden attack of stage fright, your nervous system has gone into super stressed-out mode and you need a way to be able to calm down fast. Here's a little-known trick that works every time.

To calm down almost instantly, all you have to do is defocus your eyes. That's right, just defocus your eyes. When you defocus your eyes it causes your nervous system to go into relaxation mode.

You can learn how to talk with your eyes defocused by holding your hands at the side your head at eye level. You then pay attention visually to your hands in your peripheral vision.

Practice parts of your talk while your eyes are completely defocused. Pretty soon it becomes easy to do. It becomes second nature.

Is it really that easy to stop an attack of stage fright in its tracks? Yes, it really is. *All* my students have had terrific success using this simple, easy, yet powerful technique.

Dance Together

Groups of people exhibit some very interesting dynamics, and here's one of them that you can use to your advantage.

If you were to carefully and closely watch a group of people in a seminar, you'll begin to notice a "ripple effect" when people shift position in their seats. If you were to watch the group very closely, you'll see that there will be a stillness, no one moving, then someone will shift position in their seat, followed by others around that person also shifting. It won't be the whole group at one time (unless it's a very small group). Instead it will be sections of the group where you'll see this.

You can utilize this naturally occurring phenomenon by getting into rhythm with these shifts. When you see a still section suddenly have a ripple effect, look or gesture in that direction. When another still section ripples, look or gesture in that direction. You can practice observing this dynamic when you're sitting in an audience next time. Get used to noticing these ripples of movement so you can utilize this next time you give a seminar talk.

This is a subtle yet powerfully effective way of getting into rhythm with your group. It's like you and your group are dancing together, they move and you respond.

Should You Memorize?

Should you memorize your presentation?

There are presentations I know so well, I could do them in my sleep. But, it's not that it's like an actor memorizing a script.

I suggest you do *not* memorize your seminar talks word for word. A tried and true, time-honored method of staying on track in your presentation is to simply take the main points of your talk and write them down on index cards. Then, just number the index cards in the order you plan to give your presentation.

When you're giving your seminar talk, you just start with index card number one which has the first main point (or it can be a few bullet-points) and cover that, then move on to card number two, and so on. Nice and neat, easy and effective!

Will the audience care that you have these index cards? Not in the least. Index cards are cheap, easy to carry around, and they make a terrific back-up if your presentation technology suddenly fails.

Numbering index cards gives you an inexpensive, portable, easy way to organize and present any seminar talk!

Your New Addiction

"Welcome to your new addiction!"

Sometimes just for fun, I'll start my workshops on conquering stage fright and how to do seminars with that statement.

First, I'll survey the group. "How many people here want to do seminars to promote your business, but haven't started yet because of fear of public speaking?" Some hands will go up. Then I'll say, "Welcome to your new addiction!"

Students, who at first are very hesitant to do seminar speaking due to their fear, always tell me later that after they do a few seminars, they get addicted.

It's true. I grew up painfully shy, and getting up in front of people was the last thing I thought I'd do for a living. But, it really does become addicting, and it will for you too. That is, if you're not already addicted to seminar speaking!

If you're just getting started in seminar speaking, I'd like to formally welcome you to your new addiction!

Believe Me?

How would you like to be able to come across as completely believable to your group? Do you suppose that could be useful to you?

First, it's important to remember the old expression "It's not what you say, it's how you say it." You see, your body posture and gestures are going to have a bigger impact on your audience than the actual words you speak. Study after study has shown this to be true.

So, how do you use your body posture and gestures to convey total believability? Take your hand and curl your fingers gently, letting the pad of your thumb rest naturally on the side of your index finger. (Do not make a fist!) Then, bring your hand close to your body to about the level of your solar plexus, below your chest. Your arm will naturally be shaped like an "L" in this position. This is the body posture that conveys total believability. Watch politicians, they do this all the time.

Do you think there may be times in your seminar speaking that you want to come across with an aura of total believability? Now you know how! If you want to see me demonstrate this, check out the video on *www.SeminarAcademy.com.*

Microphone, Please

If the seminar room and your audience is larger than 40 people or so, you'll likely be using a microphone. When you take questions from the audience, you may have a second mic so that when you take questions, the rest of the group can hear the question.

Never just hand someone the mic to ask questions, have an assistant hold the mic for the person asking the question. Instruct your assistant ahead of time to move away after the person poses their question. Otherwise, this person may be on the mic forever—or at least a lot longer than you wanted.

And, if you just hand the mic over to someone in the audience to ask questions, you may never get it back. Alternately, you can set up a mic on a stand and have people line up to ask one question at a time and you can announce that the limit is one question per person. This is especially useful if you're filming the event, because that way you can point one camera at the mic stand and capture all questions easily.

Don't hand the microphone over to your audience, you may never see it again.

You Are the Undisputed Expert

Let me repeat and remind you that it's not what you say, it's how you say it that counts. Numerous studies have shown that the actual words you say represent approximately 10% of the impact of your communication. The other 90% is your voice tone, your body posture, and your gestures.

It's useful, from time to time, to come across as the undisputed expert during your presentation. Here's how to convey that with your body posture and gestures.

Take one forearm and lay it across your torso, just below your chest. Your arm will form an L-shape (call that arm #1). Take the elbow of your other arm (arm #2) and rest it on top of the back of the hand of arm #1, and let the hand of arm #2 go up to your chin. Allow the fingers on the hand of arm #2 to curl gently (not a fist) and cradle your chin naturally in the space created between your thumb and index finger. Use this posture to deliver facts and data, or to handle tough questions from the audience, or whenever you need or want to convey an aura of total expertise.

It's easier to do this than to describe it, and if you want to see a video demonstration of this, you can see me demo this at *www.SeminarAcademy.com*. Go check it out!

Talk (Pause) Talk

Let me pause for a moment and talk about...pauses.

Rookie seminar speakers feel like they have to "fill space" and keep talking, talking, talking. Pauses are actually not only okay, but very powerful. There's a story of a famous stage actor who suddenly forgot his next line right in the middle of a monologue. He stood there, frozen, completely unable to recall his next line. It felt to him as if 20 minutes had passed, and he was just standing there with his mind racing, trying to recall his next line. Luckily, he finally remembered it, and kept going. After the performance, he tried to "slink away" and hide because he was so embarrassed, but he was stopped by person after person that said that his pause was one of the most powerful things they'd ever witnessed, that they were kept riveted by his dramatic pause, and the longer it went on, the more riveting and suspenseful the performance had become.

You may not need to make super-long, dramatic pauses that rivet your audience in suspense, but don't make the mistake of thinking that "dead air" is always bad.

Yes, people came to hear you speak, but you don't have to ramble on and on and on without a pause.

Judging a Book By Its Cover

You probably won't take this suggestion, but never judge if people like your presentation by how their faces look.

Obviously, there are some simple exceptions to this rule, like if people are smiling, it's pretty obvious what that means. But, it's going to happen that you're going to look out over your group and you're going to see someone with a "sour" expression on their face. You're probably going to wonder why they don't like you or what you're saying. Or you're going to see someone with their eyes closed and wonder why you're putting them to sleep.

Never, ever, decide what people are experiencing based on the look on their face. Just don't do it. I've learned this lesson over and over. One time that stands out in my mind was this one man in the front row who kept rubbing his forehead in what appeared to be a very irritated manner, shaking his head and rolling his eyes. It looked like he was hating every word that came out of my mouth. After my talk, he came up and said, "Wow, this presentation was so fantastic and I learned so much, but I only wish I didn't have this awful hangover from drinking too much last night!"

Take my advice, never judge how you're doing by the looks on people's faces!

The Bandwagon Effect

One of the group dynamics that works in your favor as a Seminar Speaker is something called "The Bandwagon Effect".

You know about the bandwagon effect, right? It's the "me too" attitude people take when they see others doing or getting something.

When I was very young, I worked at a delicatessen counter in a large supermarket. The other employees and I always scratched our heads wondering why business was either totally dead slow with no customers or we seemed to be overwhelmed with customers—never somewhere in-between. Years later I came to understand why this was.

It's a group dynamic: if someone walked up to our deli counter, other shoppers would see that person there and wonder what they were looking at and want to find out for themselves. Soon there'd be a group of people in front of the counter and other shoppers would wonder what all the commotion was about.

This is a group dynamic you want to utilize in your seminars. You want a back table where people are gathered around, booking appointments, buying products, or registering for your next big seminar, or whatever result this seminar is designed to produce.

Nervousness Be Gone!

If you're one of a number of other speakers and you're waiting your turn to speak, what should you do if you feel some nervousness or even outright fear starting to creep up on you?

Conventional wisdom would say you should go walk off your nervousness, or breathe deeply, or imagine that all the butterflies in your stomach were flying in formation. Except for that last one, maybe (just maybe) that's good advice. But I've got a suggestion that works even better.

Once I was sitting in the "green room" at a radio station. I was about to give a live radio interview and I was starting to get nervous as I thought about how many people might be listening in. I teach people all the time exactly how to overcome those kinds of jitters easily and quickly, so I knew exactly what to do: I thought of someone who, if they were going into a radio interview like this, they would not be nervous in a million years, and in fact they'd eat it up and love every minute of it. So, I pretended I was that person—I made my face just like his, I sat just like he would sit, and I adjusted my entire being to be just like him.

Nervousness gone!

That's a technique I've been teaching in my seminars for years and it really works as fast and easy as I just described. Try it!

Dress for Success

How should you dress for your seminar talk? Should you wear a suit and tie? Leather jacket and chaps? Dress shirt and slacks with no tie? A T-shirt and jeans?

As you might imagine, there's no way for me to say there's one and only one right way to dress. For sure, you'll want to take into consideration your group, your target audience, and your business or profession. If you're giving a talk to a room full of plumbers dressed in work shirts, jeans and boots, you may be better off being dressed like them, or you may want to dress up. If you're a professional person such as a real estate broker, insurance agent, financial planner, chiropractor, and so forth, you're probably going to have to dress in a suit and tie.

Some say you can never be too dressed up. Another rule of thumb is to dress at least one notch up on the dressy scale than your audience is dressed. The main factors you need to weigh are your profession or business, your target audience, your comfort, the image you're trying to portray, and who has hired you to speak, if you've been brought there by a third party.

Although I can't tell you exactly how you should or should not dress, now you have some good guidelines to help you make the best decision on how to dress.

"Always Be Prepared"

That's the Boy Scout Motto and it almost goes without saying. *Almost*. It's worth touching on simply because if you've never done seminars before, you're not aware of the many, many details that go into it. Even if you're just a guest speaker on the roster, there's still quite a large number of details to attend to. And if you are doing your own seminar, the number of details can seem mind-boggling.

You know that I suggest using a checklist to control every aspect of all phases of your seminar. Without repeating that here, my point simply is that no matter how good your plan is, no matter how good your checklist is, no matter how well you prepare, you have to be prepared for things you didn't and can't prepare for. It's just not possible to know what kind of last minute problems or difficulties will pop up.

What I'm suggesting here is a kind of "mental and emotional" preparedness above and beyond your best preparations. When unexpected problems pop up—and believe me they will—your mental attitude will be key.

Another way of saying this is "expect the unexpected." Don't let unexpected problems ruin your state of mind or seminar.

Seminars Vs. Networking

I can't knock networking as a way to build business because it works and it works well. My problem with networking is how much time and energy it chews up compared to doing seminars.

Think about it: if you go to a networking event that has 100 people, how long will it take for you to meet-and-greet all 100 people? Can you even do that? I doubt it. But even if you really work the room hard networking, how much energy will that take? How will you feel afterwards? Drained, right?

Seminar Speaking beats networking because you can talk to a room of 100 people all at one time. Afterwards, you'll feel invigorated!

When you go out networking, you have no idea if the person whose hand you just shook is a good prospect or has zero interest in what you have to offer. Sure, they may refer someone to you who is interested, but that's a long shot. On the other hand, when people come to your seminar on "How to XYZ", you know for sure that they wouldn't even be at your seminar in the first place unless they were interested in the topic of XYZ, right?

There's no better way than seminars to build business, spread your message, gain new clients, and make more money.

Seminars Vs. Networking 2

Seminar speaking makes you an expert. After all, there you are up there in front of the room talking about this topic. Not someone else. People see authors and seminar speakers in a different light. Maybe we could call it a "halo effect". When you're up there doing seminar speaking, people see you as an expert. If you have a room full of good prospects in your target market, what could be better?

On the other hand, networking doesn't give you a halo effect the way seminar speaking does. When you're out networking, it's a bit of an uphill struggle if you want to try to convince someone you're an expert at what you do.

Seminar speaking not only makes you an expert, due to the halo effect it can make you *the* expert. I can't think of a single business that can't promote and market themselves with seminars. Seminars are by far the best way to get the word out about what you do.

If you're not doing seminars yet, get started now so you can begin to reap the many rewards seminar speaking has to offer.

Door Prizes

Want a terrific and proven strategy that will help you to get people to your seminars? Simply offer door prizes as an enticement.

The best door prize is something that's not going to set you back a lot of money, but has high perceived value on the part of your target market, your seminar attendees. High perceived value to your market is absolutely key. Spending money is not mandatory. Would you like to have terrific door prizes you can get for free? Here's how:

Take some time to make a list of businesses that serve the same target market you serve, but are not in competition with you. How many of them might have something you can give away as a door prize? In other words, which businesses would be glad to reach more customers through your seminars in exchange for giving you some items to give away? You win by having valuable items to give away, and it costs you nothing. The other business wins because they inexpensively market to potential new customers.

If you're even just a little bit creative with this, you could wind up with a whole slew of valuable door prizes that cost you absolutely nothing!

A Grand Prize Drawing

In addition to offering door prizes at your seminar as I've already outlined ("Door Prizes", P. 98), also offer a grand prize drawing for some big, valuable prize. This particular prize should have high perceived value in general, or it can be something your target market finds valuable in particular. But the grand prize has to be grand in nature: the latest high tech TV, tickets for 2 to travel anywhere in the world...you get the idea. Something big that will make pretty much anyone salivate and say "Hey, I want to win that!"

This is where you'll want to affiliate with some business that serves your target market, does not compete with you, and wants to reach that market through your seminars. That business can do a tax write-off on the donation of the grand prize and they get to market their business to the local people in their target market attending your seminar. And, you already know how you win: you have a highly desired grand prize to give away, which is a big draw to get people through the door and into your seminar.

A grand prize drawing, plus door prizes, plus your irresistible seminar topic...your seminar invitation is starting to look like *the* must-attend event!

Entertainment

So far you're offering door prizes and a grand prize drawing. What about having a live band, or a magician, or a singer, or a massage therapist giving away free massages, or a comedian there as well? The general idea is this: what would your seminar attendees find fun, interesting, entertaining, or make them feel good?

For example, lets say you're a chiropractor. You could offer free five minute massages at your event to the first five people that sign up. That's just one example to get your creative juices flowing. The possibilities are endless. And you don't have to limit yourself to just one. You could have a terrific jazz combo playing after your event and a comedian doing stand-up on the breaks. The only limit to this is your imagination.

Once again, you'll get these people to appear at your seminar and do their thing at no cost to you because they get to promote themselves at no cost to them either!

Wait a second! Now you've got door prizes, plus a grand prize drawing, plus entertainment, plus your irresistible seminar topic...It sounds like you better get a bigger room to hold all the people lining up to attend your seminar!

"OK, Here's the Plan..."

Give people a general overview and the seminar "logistics" at the beginning of your seminar.

What does this mean? It means that you should, in most cases, announce basic facts like start and end times, how often you'll take breaks, where the bathrooms are located, and so forth. This is going to be generally true and necessary whether you're doing a relatively short presentation of just a few hours, but especially if you're doing an all-day or multiple-day seminar. Sure, your seminar invitation or brochure may have the start and end times clearly listed, but tell them in the beginning anyway. That will ensure that everyone is on the same page with you.

If you'll be having special "private break out" sessions, announce that. If you're taking 15 minute breaks every two hours, announce that. The idea here is to simply tell everyone how things are going to go, what the flow will be, where any other rooms are that they'll need to move to later and how to get there, and so forth.

Giving people an overview and logistics up front prevents confusion and allows people to relax and focus on your talk instead of sitting there wondering how long this thing will go, when they'll get to take a break, and so forth. You want them focusing on you and your talk, not on basic logistics you should have announced.

For the Ladies Only

Ladies, even though this is the 21st Century and all, there still sometimes may be some lingering gender bias you'll need to overcome. The "good ol' boys club" mentality can and does creep in here or there from time to time. It's a challenge to be credible and be taken seriously if you run into a "Sure, honey, go ahead and tell us what's in your pretty little head" kind of mentality.

You can overcome this in large part with your body posture. Remember that studies consistently show that the impact you make on people is largely composed of your body posture and gestures, much more than the actual words you speak. So, ladies, to project more credibility with your body posture when you stand up and speak, spread your feet to at least shoulder width or slightly wider and distribute your weight evenly on both feet. Make your stance a very solid base and don't shift your weight to only one leg. Also it's very important that your hand gestures are always palm-down facing the ground, never palm-up. A closed hand also conveys a more masculine-energy, as does a pointed index finger.

This posture and gestures project a more "masculine energy" that will help in situations where you want to be seen as more credible and believable, especially if your group is predominantly (or all) male.

For the Men Only

Guys, we naturally have and project "masculine energy" when we do seminar speaking. It's a good idea to know how to downplay this when you want to or need to, so that you don't "overpower" the ladies in your group. In other words, if your audience is mostly (or all) female, it's going to be useful to you to know how to tone down your male energy so that you don't just hammer the ladies with nothing but masculine energy.

When you decide it's appropriate to tone down the male-energy, make your hand gestures palm-up, and not palm-down, and no finger pointing or fists. Also, be sure to shift your stance so that your weight is more on one foot than the other. Don't stand with your legs spread and weight evenly on both feet. An uneven stance with palm-up hand gestures quickly tones down masculine energy. You don't have to deliver your entire talk this way, you can always switch whenever you feel it's appropriate and useful to you in the moment.

Just to be clear, there's nothing wrong with having and projecting "masculine energy", but it's good to understand how to tone that down if you want or need to. That gives you more options and better control of how your message is perceived and received by females.

YOU Make Seminars Work!

Seminar Speaking means you get your message out to a large number of prospects in a very short period of time. But if you were to ask me "David, do seminars really work that well?", then my answer would be "Seminars don't work —*you* have to make the seminar work."

It's like asking if Karate "works"; how does Karate "work" apart from the person practicing it? Karate doesn't work, it's up to the skill of the person.

Sure, seminars have the built-in power of group dynamics (like the Bandwagon Effect, for one example), but ultimately it's not seminars that work, it's *you* that makes seminars work.

Registration Sheets

Should you have a registration or sign-in sheet and have attendees sign-in as they arrive?

Personally, I'm a big fan of sign-in sheets. Are they really necessary? Certainly they're not mandatory, but I like them because they serve a number of very useful purposes.

First, a truly terrific reason to use a sign-in sheet is when you want to collect contact information on each person attending your seminar. Also, a sign-in sheet allows you to quickly review exactly who, by name, is at your seminar today. If you plan to follow up with each of your seminar attendees, the sign-in sheet makes for a nice checklist, too.

Another subtle but very powerful benefit is that by requiring everyone to sign-in, you're exerting a small but measurable amount of control over your audience before your seminar even starts. A sign-in sheet in combination with announcing logistics and ground-rules helps to prevent "seminar hijacking".

Another powerful benefit is that over time as you do more and more seminars, you can look back over past attendance "at a glance" by reviewing your file of sign-in sheets.

Make 'Em Putty in Your Hands

Here's a little known, extremely powerful presentation technique of which I became aware some years ago. Since then I've only seen a handful of seminar speakers use it. This could be considered an "advanced" presentation skill technique—not because it's difficult, because it's not. In fact, it's actually quite simple. But it does require that you are naturally funny, or know how to be funny almost on command. It's not that you have to be a stand-up comedian funny, you just have to know how to rattle off one-liners that cause a burst of laughter as well as be able to tell highly entertaining stories.

So here's the technique: alternate your presentation delivery between being funny and super-serious. A way to think about this is that your audience is alternately scared to death and then laughing their asses off.

See, I told you it was simple! But, it's easier to describe than to do. You have to be totally hilarious, and then totally serious. In the extreme, you might even be so serious as to display outright anger. This technique works especially well by telling stories in which you alternately scare them, then cause them to laugh uproariously.

What makes this technique powerful and valuable is that you've taken the audience on such an emotional roller coaster ride that they end up as practically "putty in your hands".

A Good Coach

If you wanted to become an expert golfer, who would you rather train with: Tiger Woods or his golf coach?

I hope you said his golf coach! Tiger Woods will go down in history as one of the greatest golfers ever. But, stop and think about his coach. His coach has the eagle eye to help Tiger to improve and sharpen his game. Tiger is a terrific golfer, but his coach has the skill to help Tiger hone his edge.

That's just like when my students attend my Seminar Speaking Success Mastery trainings. I have the experienced eagle eye to help you hone your skill no matter whether you're a complete rookie or a seasoned pro. Total beginners become polished pros in no time flat. Experienced speakers hone their skill and take their expertise to a whole new level.

I personally conduct each and every training. And because I always keep the group size small, each and every person gets tons of personal feedback and attention. It's one thing to be a great seminar speaker, and it's another to be able to make others great. I know exactly how to systematically take your skill to a whole new level of expertise.

Under my expert training and guidance, maybe you'll be "The Tiger Woods of Seminar Speaking Success"!

Instead of Cold Calling...

When it comes to reaching new prospects and growing your business, Seminar Speaking beats cold calling hands down.

First of all, with the ever-tightening laws and restrictions around "do not call lists" and the like, telephone cold calling may eventually go the way of the dodo bird. Cold calling is a very effective technique to generate leads, but even if there were no laws restricting it and you could just cold call like crazy, would you do it?

Most people truly hate cold calling, both face to face and over the phone. When it comes to telephone cold calling, most people suffer from "lead telephone"—that's where you sit down in front of our phone to start cold calling, but the phone just seems too heavy to pick up! And not many of us truly enjoy going out knocking on stranger's doors, either.

No, most of us truly hate any kind of cold calling. Luckily, seminar speaking comes to the rescue. Instead of forcing yourself to do cold calling you don't want to do, why not have a room full of target market prospects come to you?

Presentation Technology

If you choose to use some form of presentation technology, use it to enhance your seminar talk, not become the focus of it.

For many years, the only presentation technology in use was the overhead projector. Some people still like to use them, but I'm not a big fan. In use for many years now have been the laptop and LCD projector to display a PowerPoint presentation. Prices on both have come down significantly over the years, and I like the portability and professionalism of using that equipment.

Other technology like a handheld data device (like a cell phone) interfacing with LCD flat screens may become commonplace. If you do need or want to use presentation technology, I'd stick with the tried and true laptop and LCD set up. It's affordable, easy to use, and adds that touch of professionalism to your talk.

Technology is great if you use it to enhance your presentation, but remember that the focus of your seminar talk should be on you.

The Looping Effect

Here's an extremely slick technique to use when you have a relatively large amount of information to get across. It's called *pre-teaching*. Pre-teaching is a method of helping your seminar attendees to learn and retain information on a very deep level.

Here's how pre-teaching works. Let's say you have your information structured as a series of chunks or modules. In each module, talk about some of the information that will be coming up in a future module. It's like when you go to the movies and before the movie starts, they show you clips of movies coming out in the near future—a preview of coming attractions.

So in Module 1, you talk about and include some information you'll actually teach in Module 2 or 3. In Module 2, you talk about some information you'll actually teach in Module 3 or 4, and so on with that pattern. What this does is create a "looping effect" where every time you start a new module, the material is somewhat familiar to your group already and therefore easier to learn and remember due to repetition.

Pre-teaching is a highly effective and useful tool when you're conducting educational seminars, but you can also use it in seminars designed to sell too.

Help! I Need Somebody

Are you the type of person that urgently and sincerely wants, needs, and desires to help other people? There are a lot of people out there who, at their core, are "on a mission" to help out their fellow human beings. Let me tell you, if you're into helping people in any way, shape, or form, there is no better way to do so than seminar speaking. If you're on a mission to raise people's awareness or to show them how to overcome an illness or adversity you've already overcome, then you simply *must* do seminar speaking.

Seminar speaking allows you to get your message out to the largest possible amount of people in the shortest time span. It's exciting, and even freeing, to know that you have a tool at your fingertips that will quickly and effectively help you to get your message out to the world.

If you have a message that's going to help people, then you have no choice: you simply must get out there and do seminar speaking.

A Better Voice

Do you feel like you need to be better at speaking out loud? Do you wish you had a stronger, more confident speaking voice?

Some people really feel like they need to develop their speaking voice. They feel like their voice is not strong enough and they don't feel confident. That lack of confidence can be a real problem, even if they actually have a terrific voice.

If you want to have a stronger voice, be better at speaking out loud, and improve your confidence in your voice, I've got the solution for you.

Every day—and I mean every day—read out loud for a minimum of five minutes. What should you read? It doesn't matter. Read the newspaper, a magazine, or from a book. Don't procrastinate, just pick something and start reading out loud. Get your egg timer from your kitchen and set it for five minutes and start reading out loud. Read as if someone across the room is trying to hear what you're saying. Don't yell or strain, just imagine that you can project your voice across the room. Do this each and every day for at least five minutes.

This deceptively simple and easy technique will definitely improve your voice, strengthen your voice, and skyrocket your confidence.

No Parking Hell

Here's something that may seem obvious, but so many people overlook this that it's worth talking about.

So, you've booked your seminar, promoted it, your seminar is sold out, and the big day or night is here. You're standing there ready to start right on time, but less than half the people that registered and paid are there. Where could they all be? Your assistant reports that the parking lot is full, there's no street parking, and the rest of your seminar attendees are circling the block desperately looking for a parking space. You smack your forehead realizing you hadn't even considered the parking factor.

It can be extremely frustrating to pay for a seminar that you're eagerly looking forward to attending and then end up in a place we affectionately refer to as "no parking hell".

What kind of state of mind do you think your attendees will be in when they finally do manage to park a mile away and walk in after spending the last 20 minutes in no parking hell? And if your event is a free seminar, they might just give up and drive away, right?

Don't overlook the parking factor. Make sure your venue will have plenty of easy to find parking on the date of your event.

Adult Education Classes

Whether you're a rookie seminar speaker or an established pro, here's a tip that you can use no matter what your level of experience is.

Every couple of months or so, I receive several catalogs filled with adult education classes that are being offered. Maybe when you've received these, you've just tossed them. Or maybe you've looked through them and seen that there are classes on just about every topic you can imagine. Or maybe you've even taken some adult education classes in your community.

So, how come *you* are not one of the instructors in those catalogs? If you're a beginner, this is a great way to get your feet wet, test market your topic and your title, and practice speaking in front of people. If you're an established seminar speaker, you can expand your reach, attract more prospects, and hone your skills. And whether you're a beginner or a pro, you'll probably pick up some new clients, expand your prospect database, and make some sales.

You don't need a teaching credential or a college degree, so what are you waiting for? Make contact today and get your adult education class on your topic in the next catalog.

Two Powerful States

Here's the thing: People don't make decisions or take actions based on their intellect and rational thinking. People make decisions based on feelings and emotion. Then, once the decision has been made, they use rational thinking to justify why their decision was a good one. Here's a very simple 2-step process to influence and motivate people in your seminar speaking.

First, get them curious. Get them into a state of strong curiosity.

Then, get them into a state of intense desire. Starting with curiosity builds up a need for resolution. Then, moving them to an intense state of desire is your opportunity to link that state of desire to what you have to offer. This is a simple and easy—yet powerful and effective—series of states to lead people into.

Finally, make it easy on yourself and either tell stories that lead them into intense states of curiosity and desire, or use their naturally occurring states as they relate to your topic.

Manipulation

If you look at all the techniques I teach you that allow you to move your audience in pre-determined ways, doesn't all of that amount to nothing more than blatant manipulation? Absolutely *yes*.

First of all, anytime you get up in front of people and speak, you're going to be manipulating them just by who you are and what you say. There's no way around that. So, since you're going to be affecting and manipulating people no matter what, isn't it going to be much better if you have tools at your fingertips that allow you to be in better control of your inevitable influence?

Second—and more importantly—very often people do not take actions they should take. Very often people simply do not do what's good for them, even when they know they should. For example, how many people really eat right and exercise consistently? They know they should, but they don't. So, there you are with a product or service or message that you know will help people if only they take action on it. It's your duty to use every bit of your knowledge to "manipulate" those people to buy your stuff, use your service, or book that appointment with you.

If you don't do everything in your power to influence people to overcome their natural hesitation and inertia and to take action and do what you know will improve their life, then you are actually doing them a great disservice.

And I Quote...

How would you like to be able to quickly and easily — and even predictably — inspire, entertain, and delight your audience whenever you choose?

Here's how: *memorize quotations*. Search the web for quotes and find two or three quotes that are truly inspirational. Also, find several quotes that are truly hilarious or at least very funny.

The great thing about having several inspiring quotes and several funny quotes is that you don't have to be inspiring or funny. But, your quotations are. Whenever you need or want to lighten things up with humor, you toss out a funny quote or two. When you want to inspire your group, you toss out an inspiring quote. It's just that easy.

Memorize at least three inspiring quotes and three funny quotes. Practice delivering these quotes until you can say each one very smoothly.

If you stop and think about it, what you can do with great quotations is only limited to your imagination. Find and memorize some right now.

Confidence!

What is the number one trait and quality that you absolutely must have a seminar speaker?

Confidence! Plain and simple. You must exude an aura of confidence. Why is that so important? Because if you don't, you'll lose your audience. They won't have a good feeling about you. Confidence puts people at ease. Imagine that you were a passenger in a car and I'm the driver. If I seem unsure of myself and it looks to you like I lack confidence in my ability to drive safely, you'll want to get out of the car quickly. If I seem confident in my driving, you can relax.

You may be an expert on your topic, but people will doubt your expertise if you speak without confidence. To become a more confident speaker, simply practice your talk while you're in a strong state of confidence. One way is to recall a time when you felt super confident. The idea here is to create a link and a connection between feeling confident and being up in front of people delivering your presentation.

If you were to only develop one single quality that will make the biggest difference to you as a seminar speaker, it's confidence.

Those Damn Neighbors!

What's happening in the room next to your seminar room?

One time I did an in-house training for a company. The total number of attendees was estimated at 125 employees. My contact at the company said they didn't have a conference room large enough to accommodate a group that size, but had reserved a large room off site for us to use. The morning of the training I showed up, set up, and the large group gathered and settled in. The group turned out to be almost 150 people. I started the training and after about two minutes, without warning, a very loud band started playing next door to us. When I say loud, I mean a jet would be quiet by comparison! The worst part was that the band was terrible! My contact went off to see if somehow the band could stop playing, but word came back they had paid for their space and were going to rehearse no matter what. We even considered taking up a collection and paying them to stop playing!

If you book a venue, it's important for you to inquire as to what will be happening in the room next to you. If you don't, your entire seminar can be completely ruined.

Once Upon a Time...

One of the top techniques in terms of effectiveness and overall impact is telling stories. Perhaps it's genetically wired into us. Don't all young children at bedtime say "Tell me a story, tell me a story!"? I can easily imagine early humans gathered around a fire after cooking up the kill from a successful hunt with bellies full and eyes wide as they listen to the just-returned hunters tell their exciting tale of the hunt.

Stories always capture people's imaginations. What if you can't think of any good stories to tell from your life? Borrow stories of other people's lives. Sports stories can illustrate overcoming adversity and winning against all odds. Celebrity stories can relate passion, commitment, and motivation. Stories from history can create a wide range of emotion and reaction.

When it comes to extremely powerful seminar speaking and presentation techniques, telling stories ranks in the top ten for sure.

It's All Greek

When should you include a lot of technical terminology and jargon in your seminar speaking or presentation?

Every industry and profession has specialized terminology and jargon. There are times when jargon is not a good thing. If you're a doctor speaking to lay persons, a bunch of medical terms are going to sail right over people's heads. However, Doctor, if you're speaking to other Doctors, the terminology will probably be quite useful.

Of course, this applies to any profession and industry, not just doctors. This applies whether you're making a presentation before the board of directors, to a group of peers, or a group of prospects. The key is to "know your audience" and assess their comfort level with any jargon you're considering using in your seminar talk.

In some cases, you can use jargon they don't know to your advantage. You can cause them to get curious about some term you just tossed out, then educate them according to your plan.

Whether you use jargon or not, be sure to never lose sight of the goal you have for your seminar talk.

Considering using jargon in your seminar speaking? Follow this very simple rule of thumb: *When in doubt, leave it out!*

It's Not THAT Funny

Should you open with a joke when you do seminar speaking?

It seems like there are a lot of books on public speaking that suggest you should always open with a joke to loosen up the crowd. On the surface, there's nothing wrong with that advice. But, going below the surface, we find that this advice is very questionable.

Telling a joke right up front to a group you've never spoken to is a "make or break" proposition. If your joke is well received and everyone howls with laughter, that's great. But what if your joke is not well received for whatever reason, and they just stare at you blankly, or worse, shake their heads in disgust? To say that you have an uphill battle to recover after that is an understatement!

Another potential risk with telling a joke right off the bat is that you risk not being taken seriously after that. You could be seen as clownish.

Personally, I use a lot of off-the-cuff, impromptu humor in my talks, and most of the time it works quite well. But I don't go in with a pre-planned joke. In my opinion, it's just too risky.

Obviously, it's up to you whether or not you open with a joke, but if you do, consider yourself forewarned in case it backfires on you.

Differentiate Yourself

We are officially in the era of commoditization. Many blame the Internet (or more correctly, the World Wide Web) for this trend.

What is commoditization? It's the perception in consumers minds that one stock broker is pretty much the same as any other. One chiropractor is pretty much the same as any other. One financial planner, insurance agent, or real estate broker is the same as any other.

Along with that is the perception among consumers that since one is pretty much the same as any other, they should find the lowest possible price. The era of commoditization is the era of the consumer-driven economy. I coined the term "Wiki-World" to neatly sum up this trend.

To survive in this brave new Wiki-World, you simply must differentiate yourself from your competitors. Seminars offer you the perfect way to differentiate yourself in the marketplace. Not only are most of your competitors *not* doing seminars, but at your seminars you can create the perception of your brand and unique way of doing business.

Using the techniques I teach you here and in my Seminar Speaking Success workshops and trainings, you will definitely have the skills and abilities to survive and thrive in this brave new Wiki-World.

The Generation Gap

Credibility can be a problem for a younger business person as older more mature prospects might see the younger person as "green" and inexperienced. On the other hand, older business people run the risk of appearing behind the times and out of touch with modern ways. Worse yet, someone in middle-age runs the risk of appearing behind the times to younger prospects and inexperienced to older prospects!

Luckily, Seminar Speaking solves this problem for you no matter what your age or experience is. In your seminar talk, you can demonstrate your expertise and experience. You can display your knowledge of modern ways. Seminar speaking allows people to see that you have all of the qualities they seek in someone in your industry or profession.

Bridging the generation gap is yet another terrific benefit to doing Seminar Speaking.

Positive Mental Imagery

PMI stands for **Positive Mental Imagery**. It's the opposite of imagining failure, basically. In my workshops and trainings everyone is always very entertained by revealing the many ways people visualize bad things happening. They imagine that when they get up in front of people to speak, all kinds of things go wrong. Sometimes people intimidate themselves with their imagery, like visualizing themselves as small and looking frightened while the audience appears big and intimidating.

Instead of doing that, use your imagination to focus on positive results, like getting a standing ovation, everyone smiling and having a good time, and seeing yourself being a great speaker.

Lie back, close your eyes, take a deep breath, relax, and use PMI to create scenarios with positive results that make you feel good. Don't let your mind wander over to imagery of bad results; if that happens, steer you mind back to positive results again.

You need to condition your mind to spontaneously create PMI instead of flashing pictures of failure at you. Don't let your brain run wild and do whatever it wants. It's *your* brain!

"Smile When You Say That!"

It's easy to overlook the power of a simple smile when you're doing seminar speaking. Especially if you're a little nervous or anxious, a smile may not come naturally if your palms are sweaty and your heart is pounding. But a nice smile can actually go a long way because people really do respond to that in a positive way.

Now, I'm not talking about a giant ear to ear grin that would scare small children and houseplants. I'm talking about a nice little smile that puts people at ease.

When you smile, people tend to smile back. It's just wired into our neurology as humans. As you smile, and people smile back, you can't help but begin to start to feel good, you start to feel comfortable. Even a room full of strangers starts to look like a room full of friends when you're smiling and they're smiling back at you.

Remember to smile along the way in your seminar talk. Smile and the world smiles with you! And remember, strangers are just a bunch of friends you haven't met yet!

Understanding Does Not Cause Change

When it comes to conquering stage fright and overcoming fear of public speaking, having a new understanding is not going to change that or help one bit. This is why most "traditional advice" on dealing with stage fright simply does not work. For example, "everyone gets nervous" or "the audience wants you to succeed" are intellectual understandings that will not change a gut-level fear reaction to getting up in front of people and speaking.

This is why I teach my "inside-out" approach consisting of both visualizing positive results, and practicing your talk while feeling strong confidence to create a link between seminar speaking and feeling confident. That's my "one-two punch" that has proven to work countless times in helping people overcome fear of public speaking and conquering stage fright.

Intellectual understandings are just not enough to make a significant difference. Understanding does not cause change—the transformation has to happen on a gut-level, not just "in your head".

You Done Good

You'll never really know all the good you've done and people you've helped in your Seminar Speaking. Even if you're not doing any kind of "motivational" speaking whatsoever, you have to stop and realize that the positive impact you'll have on people and their lives is truly immeasurable. Over time, I've had people tell me right after my talk that they were impacted in a highly positive way, and I've had people years later contact me and tell me that. But think about all the people you'll never hear from whose lives you have impacted in a positive way. Even if your speaking is just getting up in front of your business associates, it's entirely possible that some off-hand comment or story you tell will touch someone's life on a deep level. Even the most mundane and ordinary settings that have nothing to do with "motivational" or "inspirational" speaking can spontaneously cause a positive impact on people.

The next time you're about to get up and speak in front of a group in any setting or context, just stop and look over the crowd and realize that at least one person is going to be positively impacted by your talk in a way you'll never even know about.

The Power of 3

Are you using the **Power of 3**?

The number three is pure magic when it comes to seminar speaking. You should be using the magical Power of 3 and here's how…

When you design your talk, figure out what are the 3 main points you want your group to walk away remembering. Near the beginning of your talk, give an overview of those 3 main points one by one. That's the first way to use the power of 3.

Next, for each of those points, set up your talk so that you preview the first point, then go into detail about that point, then close that point with a summary of that main point. Do the same with your other two main points. That's the second way you're using the power of 3.

Finally, at the very end of your talk, make sure to summarize the 3 main points you've covered. That's the third way you're using the Power of 3.

The Power of 3 is extremely useful. Don't underestimate it in your seminar speaking.

Bonus Tip:
Rocky Had Mickey...
Who's in Your Corner?

I'm certain that you know the plot of the movie *Rocky*: Rocky is a down-on-his-luck fighter who gets the chance to box the world Champion, Apollo Creed. Rocky trains for the fight alone until Mickey comes to coach and train him. With the help of Mickey, Rocky holds his own again the champion and emerges victorious.

Every public speaker possesses natural talent and learned skill. But, who is in your corner to help you hone that talent and skill so that you become, in the words of Mickey, "a very dangerous person", meaning that you are the best that you can be?

Like Rocky as he trained for the big bout, as you conduct seminars and speak in public, you will inevitably encounter obstacles along the way. Some you will overcome as if they weren't even there while others will try to stop you like a "solid right" to the jaw.

For some, a major issue is stage fright and fear of public speaking. It's a shame, because that is so easily conquered. You should not let such a small issue stand between you and your success. I realize that stage fright may seem like a big scary monster, but every single person who conquers it looks back and laughs at the idea that they were ever afraid of public speaking.

Probably one of the biggest barriers to holding semi-

nars—right after stage fright and fear of public speaking—
is the mistaken idea people have about answering questions when they're doing public speaking and seminars.
Their fear is that they'll be asked a question they either
don't know the answer to or just don't know how to handle.
Like fear of public speaking, this is a very understandable
fear—until you discover that there are many easily-learned
and quickly-mastered strategies for handling even the most
difficult and challenging questions (or even bizarre or irrelevant questions!) and easily handling questions you don't
know the answer to. Your fear quickly evaporates when you
are armed with techniques for handling *any* question that
could come your way.

Another barrier that stops many people from achiev-
ing their goals with speaking and seminars is that they've
heard that to be successful with seminars, they have to be
funny—and they don't believe they are funny. This is something that is so very easy to solve that I'm quite shocked
that anyone lets such a trifling matter stop them from putting huge amounts of money in the bank, improving their
lifestyle, and providing more for themselves and the ones
that they love. It's absolutely *not* required for you to be funny in order to achieve the desired results with your speaking and seminars. No one should ever let "I'm not funny"
stand in the way of their success.

Similarly, there are a certain percentage of people who
believe they must be able to inspire and uplift a crowd in
order to achieve success with seminars. Just like being funny, being inspirational is certainly not a pre-requisite to
seminar success.

One of the other major obstacles I find that stops people from enjoying all the income and success that speaking
and seminars bring is that they're not quite sure how to
properly structure an effective seminar presentation. This
is a very real problem in that many times business owners

think they should just get up and talk about their product or service, or educate the group about some aspect of their field of expertise, but this is a *huge* mistake. Research studies and my own direct experience conclusively shows that that informing or educating simply does *not* convert prospects into customers in a speaking or seminar setting. Many business owners are out there right now doing seminars with the deadly mistaken idea that they can get up in front of people and simply educate or inform them into becoming paying customers. Those business owners are wasting their time and money because even if they do get some meager results from those seminars, with some minor adjustments to their presentation structure, they can greatly increase their conversion rate and get dramatically better results.

Some people have tried doing a seminar or three or more in the past, but they got poor or no results, and so they conclude that seminars "don't work." This is as ridiculous as trying to ride a bicycle for the first time, failing at it, then concluding that "bicycles don't work." Ludicrous! Unfortunately, those people sometimes become so narrowly focused on those past failures that they're afraid to even try again. That is truly a shame because they deprive themselves of the single best method of marketing that ever existed and ever will exist.

All of these obstacles have one thing in common: **They deprive people of the major ongoing benefits they would receive if only they took the time to get proper information and training on how to succeed with seminars and public speaking.**

Over the course of conducting 1,893 seminars, workshops, trainings and other group events, I look back and realize that I made a lot of mistakes. Over the years, I have been personally trained and coached by some of the best and most successful seminar speakers out there. I'm certain that the biggest mistake I made was not getting that information and training sooner. I wasted a lot of time and I forfeited a large amount of income. With 20-20 hindsight, I realize now that I should never have hesitated to get the high-level information and training that would have allowed me to reach my goals much sooner.

In short, if I had taken a "Mickey" into my corner sooner in my career, I wouldn't have had my "nose" broken so many times! There are indeed a number of nuances and inside tips to making seminars the kind of resounding success that makes a person's business grow to whatever level is desired.

That's why I write books like this and train people in the art of public speaking and seminars. That's why I formed the American Seminar Academy (*www.AmericanSeminarAcademy.com*). **For speakers everywhere, at every level of skill and talent, I work to improve those skills so that every speaker can become better, can become that "dangerous person", that speaker who accomplishes his goals and becomes a star in his or her field.**

The gains that my students and clients have made *far* exceed what they could have done if merely left on their own, like Rocky did with Mickey. Without Mickey, Rockey would probably have been KO'ed within the first few rounds; but because Mickey trained and guided him, he helped Rocky through all the obstacles and potential pitfalls and made a champion of him.

I cannot urge you enough to get someone in your corner, someone who knows the ropes of public speaking and seminars, someone who can take your skill and hone it to razor-sharpness, someone who wants you to succeed in a way that is even greater than you imagined. It doesn't have to be me (although I will provide you with a few ways that you can contact me), but make sure that you have a good trainer and "corner man."

With this book, I've set before you 129 powerful ways that you can improve your seminars. Your first step to seminar speaking success is to use these tips and improve yourself. Your next step is to find a great trainer to coach you to excellence.

If you would like to contact me for information regarding the trainings that I do or other products that I have that will help you to improve you speaking success, then please use the information on the following page or complete and mail the supplied form to me. Throughout the year, I present many seminars and training sessions and I would like to keep you up-to-date about them.

Please note one thing, though: I do *not* take on just anyone as a private client nor do I accept just anyone into my small, exclusive hands-on workshop trainings. I only accept people who are positive, results-oriented people with can-do attitudes. If you are a positive, can-do person that is not afraid to "put the rubber to the road" and *make* your goals and dreams come true, then I look forward to hearing from you.

Probably the most satisfying and gratifying part of what I do is seeing and hearing about the tremendous gains people make in their business using the skills and techniques I teach them. I sincerely hope that you become one of those people.

David R. Portney has been doing trainings, keynote speeches, seminars, and every kind of public speaking you can imagine for over 22 years. He has conducted trainings and talks for major companies such the National Notary Association, The Learning Annex, and The Los Angeles Times.

David's seminars, workshops, books, manuals, and kits instruct you in many ways, including…

- how to completely conquer stage fright and eradicate public speaking fear forever.
- get the behind-the-scenes business side of things so you enjoy profits and not suffer losses.
- get the logistics of organizing your own seminars and prevent chaos and disaster.
- master expert presentation skills practically overnight so you're not fumbling around.
- exactly how to prepare and deliver a stellar presentation every time, even with little or no time to prepare.

Please contact David now to receive information about the products and services he has available that will skyrocket your seminar speaking success!

Address: The American Seminar Academy
PO Box 3555
Redondo Beach, CA 90277-1555

Web: www.AmericanSeminarAcademy.com

Email: david@seminaracademy.com

Or complete and mail the handy form on the following page! ➡

Yes! I Would Like More Information About How to Succeed in Seminar & Public Speaking!

Yes, David, please send me information about the products and services you have that will skyrocket my seminar speaking success and mail it to me at the following address:

Name: _____

Street: _____

City: _____ State/Province:_____

Zip/Postal Code: _____ Country: _____

Phone: _____

Email:_____

Please check all that apply:

☐ I am or plan to be a professional speaker.

☐ I use or plan to use seminars for my business.

☐ I speak and present seminars for my job.

Please detach this form, affix proper postage, and place in the mail

<u>or</u>

fax this application to (310) 697-3535.

llı..ıll...ıll..ıll..ı.ıll..ll.ıll.ıl.ıl..ll..ı.l

The American Seminar Academy

c/o David R. Portney

POB 3555

Redondo Beach CA 90277-1555

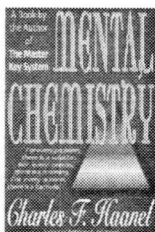

www.AmericanSeminarAcademy.com